Words of Praise for
Money-Making Investments Your Broker Doesn't Tell You About

- "At last, a complete yet easily understood guide to safety and profits from a diversified portfolio has been written. Old pro Richard Maturi provides a well-written, step-by-step explanation of highly regarded yet seldom fully explained investments. With a well-honed skill, Maturi gives readers the know-how to put profits in and take the gamble out of their one-dimensional portfolios. I guarantee it!"

> **Kenneth Coleman,**
> Editor and Publisher,
> *The Fed Tracker*

- "If you think margins are to be doodled in and convertibles are for driving, you'll want to study this book. Richard Maturi does a clear and credible job of explaining all the "other" investments most brokers can't. He demystifies options, metals, preferred stocks, short sales and other investments the big boys have always known about, and provides current phone numbers of reasonable investment alternatives. Buy it for the comprehensive financial glossary Maturi includes."

> **Linda Stern,**
> Syndicated Financial Columnist,
> Reuters

- "With so many brokers trained in and featuring manufactured, packaged, investment "products," Richard Maturi's guide to often-neglected market areas is a necessity. He covers the territory from A to Z, illuminating risks and rewards in each arena. Along the way, he spotlights investment strategies for readers in different seasons of life."

> **Donald L. Cassidy,**
> author of *It's Not What Stocks You Buy,*
> *It's When You Sell That Counts*
> and of *Plugging Into Utilities*

MONEY-MAKING
Investments

YOUR BROKER
DOESN'T
TELL YOU
ABOUT

Richard J. Maturi

PROBUS PUBLISHING COMPANY
Chicago, Illinois
Cambridge, England

ISBN 1-55738-537-8

Printed in the United States of America

BB

1 2 3 4 5 6 7 8 9 0

JB/BJS

To my mother, Bertha, and father, Mario, and my wife's parents, Muriel and Richard, who have enriched our lives and those of our children with their love and sense of family.

table of contents

9

10

preface

One of the premier tenets of successful investing lies in investment diversification, not only in terms of industry and geographical diversification, but more importantly, diversification of your investment portfolio via a range of investment opportunities.

Unfortunately, financial planners, investment brokers, and other investment counselors often offer too narrow a field of investment choices for their clients to choose from. This is not a condemnation of brokers and other investment professionals. In fact, progressive firms such as Josephthal Lyon & Ross, Inc., McDonald & Company Securities, Inc., Piper, Jaffray & Hopwood, Inc., and Prudential Securities contributed valuable information to this investment book.

But let's face the facts: your broker or financial planner is human; he or she can only absorb so much information. Nobody knows *everything* about the wealth of investment opportunities available in today's global financial markets.

We all tend to gravitate towards those areas in which we possess expertise. Since the bulk of training and experience for the vast majority of brokers and financial planners lies in the common stock, bond, and mutual fund arenas, individual investors receive most investment recommendations on individual stocks, mutual funds, and bonds.

It's a complex world out there, but you owe it to yourself and your financial future to investigate other investment opportunities which can enhance your overall investment performance.

This book will give you a firm foundation on alternative investment options which can provide greater diversification and stability to your portfolio. Don't be afraid to ask your broker questions on these alternatives and how they can fit into your overall investment strategy. They will be more than happy to help you find the right fit or at least refer you to someone who specializes in the particular area of interest.

It's your money at risk; the more informed an investor you become, the better your broker or financial planner can serve you. It is a win/win situation for all involved.

Richard J. Maturi
Cheyenne, Wyoming

acknowledgments

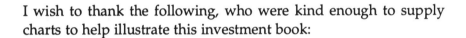

I wish to thank the following, who were kind enough to supply charts to help illustrate this investment book:

Investor's Business Daily
McDonald & Company Securities, Inc.
The Bank of New York
Value Line Investment Survey

1

the importance of diversification techniques

TYPES OF DIVERSIFICATION

As indicated in the preface to this investment book, diversification ranks as a key element in the successful investing equation. There's a wide variety of theories and strategies on how best to achieve diversification and we will delve into the thoughts behind each of them.

First of all, it is important to recognize that diversification can take several forms. Even more important, your diversification strategy needs to be adjusted or realigned from time-to-time. To be sure, you don't just adopt any plan and stick with it forever and ever.

After all, the economic world continues to change and evolve, running through economic and political cycles that, in turn, end up reflected in the financial markets. Likewise, the variety of asset classes, financial instruments, geographical locations, companies and industries, and investment options react differently during changing economic scenarios, or from one scenario to another.

For example, precious metals have traditionally performed well during periods of high inflation (as evidenced in the 1970s) and investor lack of confidence, and fared less well during periods of prosperity and stable economic and political scenarios.

Inherent in all diversification strategies is the desire to avoid the risks associated with having "all your eggs in one basket" and then having that basket turned upside down by changing economic forces.

Diversification provides protection against a variety of investment risks such as: economic and industry cycles; technological change adversely affecting a particular company or industry; geographical recessions or contractions; interest rate risk; natural, political, and economic crises; changes in raw materials supplies; and plain old management miscalculations and blunders.

As mentioned earlier, diversification can be effectively accomplished through a variety of investing techniques and, more likely, a combination of techniques designed to reduce risk from investing in too narrow a range of investment options.

Company Diversification

The most obvious method of adding breadth to your investment portfolio is to avoid risking all of your available financial resources on one company, no matter how much faith you have in that company. Like betting all of your savings on one horse, you run the risk that your "horse" will stumble, leaving you with substantial losses or even a total loss.

For years, International Business Machines Corporation (NYSE: IBM), headquartered in Armonk, New York, was touted as one of the premier "Blue Chip" American companies, the stock to own for decades to come.

To be sure, IBM had compiled an enviable track record. From 1976 to 1985, earnings advanced from less than $4 per share to over $10.50 per share. Investors shared in the good fortunes of the information processing giant. Dividends rose from $3.44 per share from 1981 to $4.40 per share in 1987. During that same time frame, IBM's stock price surged from a low around $48 1/2 per share to over $175 per share in 1987, just preceding that year's October stock market crash.

It looked like it would go on forever. Then reality hit. For far too many years, IBM failed to properly react to changing market conditions. Businesses were moving away from mainframe computers (IBM's major strength) to the ever more powerful personal computers and PC-based information networking systems. As a result, earnings stumbled to $3.69 per share in 1991 and IBM's stock price plummeted to less than $46 per share by mid-1993.

Anyone who would have invested their whole nest egg in IBM stock during that time period would have witnessed their investment portfolio drop to less than a fourth of its former value in a few years. It doesn't take a brain surgeon to understand the importance of diversifying his or her investment purchases among different companies.

INDUSTRY DIVERSIFICATION

Just as individual companies and their stocks can run into trouble and fall out of favor with investors, whole industries can encounter turbulent times when company and industry revenues and earnings decline drastically and company stock prices experience very steep declines.

Industry fallout occurs for a host of reasons. Cyclical industries such as automobile, metals, paper products, and steel undergo periodic economic cycles as the economy expands and contracts.

As the economy starts to turn upward off the bottom of a recession or stagnant period, cyclical stocks start to come back to life and represent one of the best investment opportunities around. Unfortunately, as the economy and business cycle mature, cyclical stocks begin to lose steam, eventually falling out of favor again as earnings start to taper off at first and then decline. It's a great ride up but like a roller coaster, the trip down can be more than a little bit harrowing.

To illustrate, let's take a look at the general steel industry. A little sleuthing in *The Value Line Investment Survey* uncovers important composite statistics. Steel revenues stood at $2,619 million in 1988, improving to $3,381.7 million in 1990 before starting to flatten out with an uncertain economy.

Industry net profit jumped more than 11 percent between 1988 and 1990 and then declined in 1991. Steel company stocks also rode the cycle, rising from the end of 1987 to peak out in 1989.

Typical of the overall steel industry, Birmingham, Alabama's Birmingham Steel Corporation (NYSE: BIR) earnings rose from $1.07 per share in 1987 to $3.25 per share in 1989 then dropped to $1.76 per share in 1990 and 60 cents per share in 1991. The company's stock price followed suit rising to nearly $30 per share in 1989 from a low of a tad over $10 per share in 1987. The faltering economy put the skids on earnings and Birmingham's stock price which bottomed out in 1990 at $10 1/2 per share. (See Figure 1–1, Birmingham Steel Corporation).

A review of other general steel industry stocks exhibit similar trends with slightly different timing of earnings and stock price declines. The same basic patterns, with little exception, can be found in other cyclical market segments.

Suffice it to say, investing heavily in a single industry exposes your portfolio to significant risks and investment losses in the event the economy starts to sour.

Another way that industries can suffer investor apprehension and declining stock prices arises from changes in the balance of the world power structure. In the wake of the fall of the Berlin Wall, opening up of Eastern Europe, disintegration of the U.S.S.R. and communism worldwide, and successful peace accord, economic prospects for defense firms and many of the companies serving the military market evaporated almost overnight.

Of course, the more diversified companies and ones that could easily shift from military products to commercial product lines and services were able to thwart some of the economic blow

Figure 1–1
BIRMINGHAM STEEL CORPORATION

BIRMINGHAM STEEL NYSE-BIR | RECENT PRICE **23** | P/E RATIO **23.5** (Trailing: 29.0 Median: NMF) | RELATIVE P/E RATIO **1.49** | DIV'D YLD **1.9%** | VALUE LINE **605**

TIMELINESS **4** Below Average (Relative Price Performance Next 12 Mos.)
SAFETY **3** Average (Scale: 1 Highest to 5 Lowest)
BETA 1.10 (1.00 = Market)

High: 5.5 9.0 12.4 16.7 19.9 18.8 15.7 25.8 27.8
Low: 5.2 5.5 6.8 8.6 13.8 7.0 8.4 13.6 21.0

Target Price Range 1996 1997 1998

7.5 x "Cash Flow" p'sh — 3-for-2 split — 3-for-2 split

1996-98 PROJECTIONS

	Price	Gain	Ann'l Total Return
High	50	(+115%)	23%
Low	30	(+30%)	9%

Insider Decisions

	J	A	S	O	N	D	J	F	M
to Buy	0	0	0	0	0	0	0	0	0
Options	0	0	0	0	0	2	0	0	0
to Sell	0	0	0	0	0	0	0	0	0

Relative Price Strength

Shaded areas indicate recessions

Institutional Decisions

	1Q93	2Q93	3Q93
to Buy	44	52	45
to Sell	30	38	52
Hld's(000)	16554	16145	15672

Percent shares traded 15.0 / 10.0 / 5.0

Options: NYSE

1977	1978	1979	1980	1981	1982	1983	1984	1985	1986	1987	1988	1989	1990	1991	1992	1993	1994	© VALUE LINE PUB., INC.	96-98
--	--	--	--	--	--	--	--	27.08	9.24	13.28	18.56	23.85	23.82	21.95	18.47	21.15	23.60	Sales per sh^A	36.30
--	--	--	--	--	--	--	--	1.52	.86	1.29	1.90	2.84	1.95	1.15	1.62	1.50	2.60	"Cash Flow" per sh	4.65
--	--	--	--	--	--	--	--	.55	.60	.72	1.53	2.17	1.17	.40	1.11	.65	1.70	Earnings per sh^B	3.60
--	--	--	--	--	--	--	--	--	--	--	.12	.27	.33	.33	.33	.33	.40	Div'ds Decl'd per sh^C	.75
--	--	--	--	--	--	--	--	6.48	.80	1.81	2.23	1.17	1.92	1.03	2.48	2.80	2.35	Cap'l Spending per sh	3.70
--	--	--	--	--	--	--	--	1.79	3.30	4.03	5.92	7.81	8.12	7.20	9.49	10.55	11.70	Book Value per sh^D	17.70
--	--	--	--	--	--	--	--	3.37	16.43	16.43	18.53	18.57	18.57	22.61	21.30	21.40		Common Shs Outst'g^E	21.50
--	--	--	--	--	--	--	--	11.5	12.1	7.2	7.3	12.8	24.1	12.9	Bold figures are			Avg Ann'l P/E Ratio	11.0
--	--	--	--	--	--	--	--	.78	.81	.60	.55	.95	1.54	.78	Value Line			Relative P/E Ratio	.85
--	--	--	--	--	--	--	--	--	--	1.1%	1.7%	2.2%	3.5%	2.3%	estimates			Avg Ann'l Div'd Yield	1.9%

CAPITAL STRUCTURE as of 3/31/93
Total Debt $148.9 mill. Due in 5 Yrs $35.7 mill.
LT Debt $90.1 mill. LT Interest $8.6 mill.
Incl. $13.0 mill. capitalized leases.

(LT interest earned: 3.5x; total interest coverage: 2.9x) (29% of Cap'l)
Leases, Uncapitalized Annual rentals $.7 mill.
Pension Liability None - No defined benefit plan
Pfd Stock None

Common Stock 21,396,352 shs. (71% of Cap'l) as of 5/13/93

							91.4	151.8	218.1	343.8	443.0	442.5	407.7	417.7	450	505	Sales ($mill)^A	780
							12.0%	17.2%	16.9%	15.8%	18.9%	12.7%	9.1%	13.2%	12.0%	17.0%	Operating Margin	19.5%
							3.3	6.3	9.5	10.4	12.6	14.8	14.5	16.8	18.5	19.0	Depreciation ($mill)	23.0
							1.9	7.9	11.7	24.7	40.2	21.5	6.9	19.9	14.0	36.0	Net Profit ($mill)	77.0
							50.3%	49.0%	45.5%	37.0%	36.9%	37.5%	27.8%	38.3%	39.0%	38.0%	Income Tax Rate	38.0%
							2.0%	5.2%	5.4%	7.2%	9.1%	4.9%	1.7%	4.8%	3.1%	7.2%	Net Profit Margin	9.8%
							16.9	25.7	42.7	15.2	32.9	21.8	34.6	74.5	45.0	50.0	Working Cap'l ($mill)	110
							49.0	61.5	79.1	39.8	31.0	27.2	98.4	93.7	91.0	100	Long-Term Debt ($mill)	105
							6.1	54.2	66.3	109.6	145.0	150.8	133.8	214.6	225	250	Net Worth ($mill)	380
							7.0%	8.7%	10.1%	18.4%	23.7%	12.8%	4.9%	7.9%	6.0%	11.5%	% Earned Total Cap'l	17.0%
							30.7%	14.5%	17.7%	22.5%	27.7%	14.3%	5.2%	9.3%	6.0%	14.5%	% Earned Net Worth	20.0%
							30.7%	14.5%	17.7%	20.7%	24.3%	10.2%	.8%	6.5%	3.0%	11.0%	% Retained to Comm Eq	16.0%
							--	--	--	8%	12%	28%	84%	30%	51%	24%	% All Div'ds to Net Prof	21%

brought about by changed world conditions, assuming those alternative markets remained healthy.

Falls Church, Virginia-based General Dynamics Corporation (NYSE: GD), as the nation's second largest supplier of military equipment including aircraft, missiles, launch vehicles, submarines, and tanks, was hit hard by the breakout of peace. The company showed a hefty loss of $15.34 per share in 1990 from a gain of $7.01 per share a year earlier and revenues dropped from over $10 billion in 1990 to just over $6 billion estimated for 1993.

General Dynamics' stock also reacted as though hit by one of its own missiles, sinking from a 1989 high of $60 1/2 per share to a low of $19 per share in 1990.

Management efforts to shed noncore businesses have worked to improve prospects for the defense contractor, but it remains to be seen how proposed military cutbacks under the Clinton Administration will play out over the long-term.

Domestic political events can also negatively impact the future prospects of portions of or even whole market sectors. For example, uncertainties over proposed healthcare reforms and changes in national energy policies worked to put healthcare stocks and some energy and utility stocks in turmoil in 1993.

To illustrate, from January 1, 1993 through June 27, 1993, the Medical/Healthcare Index declined more than 12 percent while healthcare reform trial balloons were floated by the Clinton Administration. (See Figure 1–2, Medical/Healthcare Index.)

One of the index composite stocks, Johnson & Johnson Company (NYSE: JNJ) was hit by the epidemic of healthcare worries.

Figure 1–2
MEDICAL/HEALTHCARE INDEX

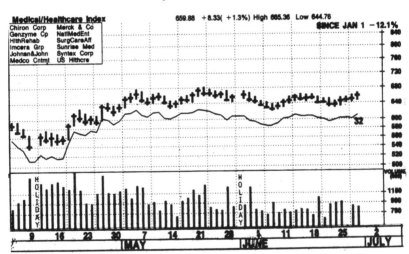

Source: *Investor's Business Daily.*
Reprint with permission of *Investor's Business Daily,* June 1993.

A leading manufacturer of health care products such as baby, dental, first aid, medical equipment, pharmaceuticals, surgical products, and toiletries; New Brunswick, New Jersey-based Johnson & Johnson, saw its stock drop from a 1992 high of nearly $59 per share to $42 per share at the end of June 1993. The stock price decline occurred despite higher projected 1993 revenues and earnings.

Not only is it wise to diversify your investment by industry, it makes good sense to keep a close pulse on industry health and the economic, political, and other factors which can wreak havoc with revenues and earnings.

GEOGRAPHICAL DIVERSIFICATION

Until this past decade, geographical diversification meant spreading your investments across geographic and economic sectors of the United States, and possibly a rare venture into Canadian investment opportunities.

With the proliferation of foreign stocks listed and traded on U.S. stock exchanges and in the over-the-counter market in recent years, in the form of American Depositary Receipts (ADRs) (see Chapter Two, for an in-depth discussion of American Depositary Receipts), the choice of owning foreign stocks and distributing your investments geographically is virtually limitless. Today, global diversification is as easy as picking up the phone and calling your broker.

In addition to the direct purchase of ADRs, mutual fund companies have launched literally hundreds of single country, international region, and global funds to whet the appetite of even the most stay-at-home investor.

Just to list a few, you can choose from Alliance New Europe, DFA Group: Japan Small Company, Eaton Vance China Growth, Merrill Lynch Latin America, Mexico Fund, and, Templeton Worldwide.

DIVERSIFIED COMPANIES

It's even possible to attain a degree of diversification within a single company by investigating how diverse its operations are. This internal diversification can take several forms. The company could sport a broad line of products and services crossing several industries or that react oppositely to economic cycles.

Hillenbrand Industries, Inc. (NYSE: HB), headquartered in Batesville, Indiana, spreads its operations over several industries ranging from caskets (Batesville Casket Company) to hospital beds, stretchers, etc., (Hill-Rom Company) to luggage and equipment cases (American Tourister). Other Hillenbrand segments sell funeral insurance and manufacture high security locks. With the proliferation of gaming across the United States, the firm also has an interest in a Deadwood, South Dakota casino.

The strategy appears to be paying off handsomely. From 1989 through 1992, Hillenbrand's revenues jumped nearly $300 million. Earnings followed suit, surging more than 50 percent to $1.62 per share in fiscal 1992 from $1.01 per share in fiscal 1989 ended November 30th.

Investors paid close attention to Hillenbrand's success story. From a stock price of a little over $13 per share in 1989, the firm's stock rose to an all-time high of $48 5/8 per share before pulling back to $42 1/2 per share in mid-1993. (See Figure 1–3, Hillenbrand Industries, Inc.).

Hillenbrand's product lines also vary in the way they react to economic cycles. The casket business is virtually recession-proof while the firm's move into gaming can take advantage of more prosperous economic times, expanding personal disposable income and rising trends in leisure spending.

A company can also diversify geographically with sales branches, facilities, and other operations in various regions of the United States or with overseas operations and sales facilities.

Battle Creek, Michigan-based Kellogg Company (NYSE: K), the world's largest manufacturer of ready-to-eat cereals garners over 40 percent of annual revenues from foreign operations. With overseas cereal markets growing faster than the domestic United

Figure 1–3
HILLENBRAND INDUSTRIES, INC.

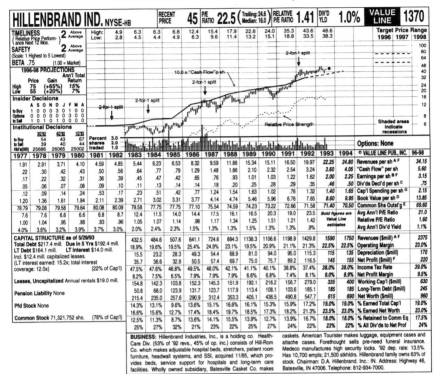

States market, Kellogg is well-positioned to benefit from expanding foreign opportunities despite a maturing of the U.S. market. With a commanding position in most international markets, Kellogg promises to deliver higher revenues and earnings at least through the 1990s.

The Molson Companies, Ltd. (TSE: MOLA.TO) represents an excellent example of a company dividing its operations both geographically and along product lines. Based in Toronto, Ontario; the Canadian company claims over 50 percent of the Canadian beer market, ranks as the second largest importer of beer into the gigantic United States market, and targets major inroads into overseas markets such as Australia, The Netherlands, the United Kingdom, Germany and Japan by forming strategic relationships with foreign brewers.

In addition, Molson rounds out its product line with a group of more than 200 owned, franchised, or affiliated retail home remodeling stores (most under the Beaver Lumber umbrella) and DuBois Chemicals, a growing player in the large worldwide specialty chemicals arena.

Despite a recessionary economy, Molson has continued to post higher earnings per share every year since fiscal 1986. With a return to a better economic climate, Molson's earnings are poised to takeoff.

Advice on Strategies

Every investor needs to assess his or her risk tolerance in determining an investment strategy. A diversification strategy that may be comfortable for one investor may give another investor many sleepless nights.

You need to thoroughly examine your risk posture before you undertake defining and implementing your investment strategy. It's a crucial element in successful investing.

Within the framework of specific risk tolerances, you can construct your investment strategy and portfolio. It's also important to remember that your risk tolerance changes as your financial circumstances, age, family obligations, and anticipated capital requirements change overtime.

A young person has more time to recoup from investment setbacks and can take on a more aggressive stance in developing a portfolio mix. On the other hand, a retired person requiring an income stream from current investments to meet ongoing living expenses probably needs to establish a more conservative investment stance.

Some investors choose to position their portfolio holdings based on expected economic scenarios, shifting their investment mix accordingly. For example, a portfolio of high-quality income stocks and bonds may form the majority of their investment position during recessionary times while the bulk of their portfolio during a business upturn may consist of cyclical stocks on the verge of a rebound.

LIFE CYCLE DIVERSIFICATION

As mentioned above, your financial situation changes drastically over the years. As a single, young rising executive or budding entrepreneur, your financial situation is extremely different than when you have a spouse and growing family obligations. Initially, college financing will take precedence followed by higher income and retirement years, with the possible need of accumulating wealth for larger medical expenses and long-term health care responsibilities.

All of these changes need to be anticipated when building an investment portfolio. With longer life spans and corresponding requirements for a larger nest egg to last out those extended retirement years, there's been good reason to readdress investment portfolios, risk postures, and overall investment strategies to meet those additional financial obligations.

Likewise, the emergence of the sandwich generation (those parents which have taken care of their children and now face the responsibility of years of taking care of their own parents) places additional financial burden on today's investors. The trend toward children returning home after graduating from college or entering the workforce, in order to help make ends meet in today's tough economic environment, also adds new financial considerations which simply did not exist just a few short years ago.

Life cycle theory looks at these life stages and proposes model portfolios designed to achieve the desired performance goals to meet anticipated financial obligations within specific risk parameters.

According to life cycle investing theory, individuals progress through different life cycle stages with vastly different investment goals and risk tolerances associated with them. For the average investor, without taking into account the life cycle approach, the risk/return relationship would be reflected as shown in Figure 1–4, Risk/Return Relationship. Each investor would need to determine for him- or herself how much risk they want to assume to achieve greater returns, as indicated by a shift to the right on the risk/return line.

Typically, younger investors would adopt a higher risk posture to earn higher returns and build up their wealth (Point A). If they incur losses during this earlier stage of their lifecycle, they have time to recoup with subsequent investments. On the other hand, older investors tend to gravitate toward the lower end of the risk/return relationship (Point B), desiring to preserve existing wealth and its income stream. In addition, their investment stance would be tempered from memory of loss experience occurring in earlier years.

Inherent in life cycle investing is the premise that certain types of investments and risk postures are more favorable for certain stages of investors' lives. This theory also recognizes the importance of early investment planning and the anticipation of future financial commitments and cash outflows (such as college

Figure 1–4
RISK/RETURN RELATIONSHIP

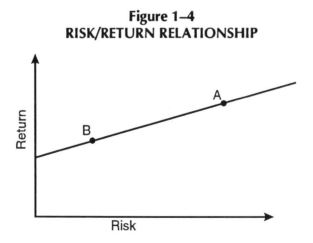

Source: Richard J. Maturi, *Divining the Dow* (Probus, 1993).

tuition expenses). Finally, it emphasizes the importance of remaining flexible enough to make the appropriate investment mix adjustments as the investor progresses from one life cycle to the next.

Four phases comprise the life cycle. Each phase and its related characteristics are noted in Figure 1–5, Life Cycle Phases and Characteristics. As you move through your life cycles, you also move from accumulation (early career), to consolidation

Figure 1–5
LIFE CYCLE PHASES AND CHARACTERISTICS

Phase	Characteristics
Accumulation	Early career. Small net worth, large liabilities such as house mortgage and credit purchases, illiquid assets. Priorities include accumulating savings for new home, college expenses, etc. Higher risk posture with long-term investment horizon. (Point A)
Consolidation	Mid-to-late career. Best income earning years coupled with declining expenses as children leave home and house expenses taper off. Peak wealth accumulation years. Institution of more risk control to protect built-up capital. (Point B)
Spending	Retirement years. Financially independent status. Accumulated assets cover living expenses. Low-risk posture to conserve and protect assets for income generation. (Point C)
Gifting	Realization that accumulated assets exceed anticipated living expenses. Redirection of assets to provide for heirs or other causes. Still low-risk posture to ensure passing along assets with the exception that some people at this phase take on pet projects without regard to the amount of risk involved.

Source: Richard J. Maturi, *Divining the Dow* (Probus, 1993).

(mid-to-late career) to the spending and gifting stage (late career through retirement).

Key factors to focus on as you move through your life cycles are stability of principal, current income requirements, capital growth, aggressive income, and risk tolerance.

Principal stability occurs by searching out investments that provide optimum protection against market loss and valuation fluctuations. While this type of investment will earn a degree of return, its primary task remains to guard against loss of principal.

Current income generating investments such as certificates of deposits, Treasury bills and bonds, corporate bonds, and dividend paying common and preferred stocks typically take on more importance in the portfolio as the individual advances through the life cycle phases.

Capital growth investments seek long-term capital appreciation to build the desired level of wealth to meet future financial obligations. It's important to start your investment plan early in order to have adequate time to accumulate your nest egg. The earlier you begin your savings and investment portfolio, the longer the miracle of compounding has to work for you.

Compounding works like this. Let's assume you own a stock that yields 10 percent annually. In ten years, you would earn back your original investment. However, if you were savvy enough to reinvest your cash dividends [through a dividend reinvestment program (DRIP), for example] in company stock, you would shave two years and seven months off the time required to earn back your original investment outlay. Not a bad deal for holding off from using those cash dividends as they are earned.

Aggressive income and growth investments combine higher potential returns with a greater degree of risk and are appropriate for those individuals in the accumulation phase of the life cycle.

Diversification Rule of Eight

One of the proposed diversification strategies, the "Rule of Eight," contends that a minimum of eight stocks is required to properly achieve enough protection to prevent the occurrence of an unpredictable event to any single stock from devastating the overall value of your investment portfolio.

Numerous risks can impact the market performance of any stock. Prolonged labor unrest, natural disasters, technological advances, fraud, unfavorable legislation are but a few of the misfortunes which can cause a firm's operating and financial performance to falter, sinking the company's stock price in the process.

While any of these events can happen to any one of the companies in which you own shares, statistics tell us that the odds of them happening to more than one at the same time is greatly reduced through proper diversification.

Therefore, limiting the amount of money, by aggregate or percentage, invested in any one stock or investment ranks as a top investment strategy and wealth preserver.

Diversification Through Cluster Investing

John Slatter, a senior vice president at Hickory Investment Advisors in Cleveland, Ohio and author of *Safe Investing* (New York Institute of Finance, 1991) discusses achieving diversification through cluster investing.

"Cluster investing does not receive much attention but should be considered by investors," says Slatter.

According to Slatter, even though there are approximately 75 different industries to choose from, it is possible for you to invest in 10 to a dozen stocks (each in a separate industry) and still not be properly diversified.

How is this possible? This can occur because your stock holdings might be situated in only one or two clusters. For example, you can locate 10–15 growth stocks, all in different industries, but within a single cluster, the growth stock cluster.

In the event the growth stock sector of the market retreats, even as the rest of the market advances, your portfolio could suffer a major decrease in value.

You can also fall into the utility cluster trap. Even though you purchase a variety of different utility stocks (electric, gas, telephone, and water), you have not successfully diversified outside of the utility cluster even with the variety of utility types and a slew of different geographic locations.

The trick is to spread out your stock purchases into a variety of clusters. Slatter defines a cluster as a group of issues which possess something in common, particularly their market action. Thus, the growth cluster can contain stocks in very distinct basic industries such as Procter & Gamble Company (consumer products), Hillenbrand Industries, Inc. (caskets, hospital equipment, and luggage and equipment cases), and Emerson Electric Company (electrical and electronic products and systems).

Slatter identifies five clusters: basic industries, consumer/cyclical, growth, oil and related, and utilities. Constructing a portfolio with a representation in each of the five clusters promises to reduce your investment risk and deliver better performance. Of course, you can adjust the percentages invested in each of the five clusters as economic and market conditions dictate.

ASSET ALLOCATION

"If you can position yourself in the right asset categories and do just a reasonable job of picking the right stocks or bonds, you can improve your performance. Getting situated in the right asset categories offsets a great many mistakes in individual stock picking," says Bradley E. Turner, director of McDonald & Company Securities, Inc.'s Gradison-McDonald Asset Management segment in Cincinnati, Ohio.

According to Turner, you need to take into consideration your own risk tolerance and investment time horizon when setting your investment objective and asset allocation strategies.

"If your investment objective is income versus total return or aggressive growth, your asset allocation mix will differ substantially from that constructed for the other two objectives," says Turner.

Figure 1–6, Asset Allocations illustrates the McDonald & Company Securities, Inc. long-term model allocations for the income, total-return, and aggressive investor. These recommended asset allocation models are for long-term investors with at least a five-year time horizon.

"Unfortunately, few individuals construct their portfolios within the framework of a sensible, preestablished investment policy or strategy. Most portfolios tend to be product-driven (individual stock, bonds, or other investments) versus strategy driven, resulting in portfolios that are both inappropriate to achieve desired investment objectives and unprofitable," warns Turner.

"Taking the time to define your investment goals and following through with well-researched and thought-out asset allocation and securities selection consistent with your goals can help you develop a portfolio both appropriate and profitable," he adds.

Simply stated, asset allocation seeks to minimize investment risk with a spreading of portfolio assets among different investment alternatives.

Given an investor's risk tolerance and investment goals, an asset allocation strategy can be constructed to deliver the desired return within the established risk parameters. The asset allocation method uses normal ranges for each class of investment and adjusts the portfolio as required to maintain the desired balance and take advantage of unique investment opportunities. The allocation ranges vary depending on the individual investor's risk tolerance, investment goals, age, and financial circumstances.

For a graphic presentation of the asset allocation strategy as discussed above, refer to Figure 1–7, Asset Allocation Pyramid. It cannot be stressed too much: investors need to take into account their age, need for liquidity, financial circumstances, tax situation, risk tolerance, and investment goals in the construction of their own asset allocation pyramid and strategy.

For example, a young couple would need a heavier weighting of growth stocks to accumulate a nest egg to finance their

Figure 1–6
ASSET ALLOCATIONS

INCOME

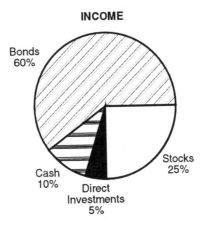

Bonds
60%

Stocks
25%

Cash
10%

Direct
Investments
5%

TOTAL RETURN

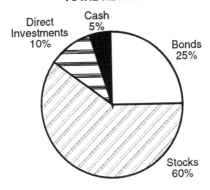

Direct
Investments
10%

Cash
5%

Bonds
25%

Stocks
60%

AGGRESSIVE

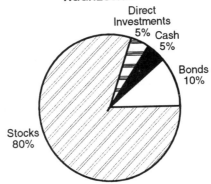

Direct
Investments
5% Cash
5%

Bonds
10%

Stocks
80%

Source: McDonald & Company Securities, Inc.

Figure 1–7
ASSET ALLOCATION PYRAMID

Source: Richard J. Maturi, *Divining the Dow* (Probus, 1993).

children's college expenses, acquire wealth to purchase a larger home, and build net worth for their retirement years. They can afford to take on higher risk at this stage of their lives because they have ample time to recoup any losses.

At the opposite extreme, investors already in their retirement years need to concentrate on safety of principal and protecting their current income flow to meet on-going living expenses. They can no longer afford to face volatile market risks in pursuit of higher than normal investment returns. In this instance, a portfolio stressing safety and income could be constructed from a mixture more heavily weighted in fixed income securities with smaller proportions of equities, and cash and cash equivalents.

The basic variable ratio plan for asset allocation consists of developing upper and lower limits for each type of investment. According to theory, the ideal ratio plan would provide minimum stock holdings at market peaks and maximum stock holdings at market bottoms.

Adding to and reducing positions in each category occurs when the percentage of holdings in a particular classification moves outside of a channel at certain intervals from the median. For example, a strategy may start to reduce the stock portion of the asset allocation portfolio by five percent when it rises 10 percent above its median level and increase its stock segment by five percent when it falls 10 percent below its median level.

By initiating asset shifts at specified intervals, the variable ratio plan offers better protection against being too heavily invested in one type as can occur under a constant ratio or constant dollar asset allocation approach. For example, the two constant strategies result in the same percentage of stocks being held whether the market is approaching a top or nearing a bottom, increasing the risks of incurring substantial losses and missing profit opportunities. Considering that the purpose of the asset allocation approach to investing is to increase total return and reduce risk, the variable ratio plan offers more flexibility, safety, and a bigger opportunity for better than normal investment performance.

THE NATIONAL ASSESSMENT MANAGEMENT (NAM) APPROACH

National Assessment Management Corporation, an investment counselor in Louisville, Kentucky has been employing variable asset management for decades with impressive results. I first ran across the company when I covered its parent, First Kentucky National (First National Bank of Louisville and now part of National City Corporation, a bank holding company headquartered in Cleveland, Ohio) for *OTC Review* (now *Equities*) in June 1987.

In the December 1987 issue of *Institutional Investor*, I wrote an article on First Kentucky Company (now National Asset Management Company) as part of a feature on four regional bank investment management operations that achieved enviable track records. In November, 1991, *Institutional Investor* wrote a follow-up article on National Asset Management titled, "Louisville Slugger."

Personally, I like National Asset Management's investment philosophy as evidenced in the *Institutional Investor* article quote by Irvin W. Quesenberry, Jr., managing director and principal of NAM, "We don't talk quartiles. We talk long-term relationships. No farmer pulls up his damn radishes everyday to see how they are growing."

NAM strives to add value relative to the Standard & Poors 500 (S&P 500) by screening equities with superior attributes for low P/E, high yield, and value growth. Figure 1–8, Screening Criteria illustrates primary and secondary criteria screening attributes.

During the five-year period ended December 31, 1992, NAM outperformed the S&P 500 in up markets, 28.2 percent versus 23.9 percent (1/88 to 12/89) and 22.8 percent versus 20.7 percent

Figure 1–8
SCREENING CRITERIA

	Low P/E	High Yield	Value Growth
Primary Criteria	• 20% below market	• 20% above market	• 10% average annual EPS growth (5 year) • No decline in annual EPS last 5 years
Second Criteria	• Minimum ROE of 10% (1 year)	• Dividend increase 6 of last 10 years • Minimum ROE of 10% (1 year)	• Debt/% Cap < 40% • EPS increased last quarter and 12 months • Minimum ROE of 13% (1 year)

Source: National Asset Management Corporation.

(10/90 to 12/92). Likewise, NAM outperformed the S&P 500 in the down market (1/90 to 9/90) turning in a –7.8 percent performance compared with –11.1 percent for the S&P 500.

A key component of the NAM investment management approach lies within variable asset allocation.

"It takes the timing and guesswork out of the equation. Our own 20-year study of rebalancing our asset mix five percent when it moves outside of the normal range reflects we can achieve approximately the same annual return but substantially reduce the risk. By rebalancing, we force ourselves to take profits in rising markets and thus, reduce our exposure to a downturn," says Quesenberry.

For example, by rebalancing the portfolio as required by set parameters, NAM ended up with a 51 percent equity exposure at the end of the 20 year period, well within its acceptable risk tolerance. On the other hand, if the portfolio had not been rebalanced periodically, it would have ended up with an equity exposure of 77 percent, adding substantially to the risk posture of the portfolio.

H.D. VEST ASSET ALLOCATION FINDINGS

H. D. Vest Financial Services, Inc. in Irving, Texas, has compiled extensive research on the benefits of asset allocation.

Too often, most investors believe they have the greatest degree of control over financial risk by paying strict attention to individual security selection. According to Vest, a 1986 study by Brinson, Beebower and Hood demonstrated exactly the opposite. This study showed that 95 percent of the long-term portfolio returns were attributed to the investment categories versus either the security selection or the timing of investment transactions.

A 1989 H. D. Vest Financial Services study confirms the multiple asset allocation approach. That landmark study tracked total returns from several asset categories over a 20-year period that covered economic cycles ranging from recession to growth to inflation. The profits from the various asset classes were reapportioned annually to conform with the multi-asset portfolio's original targeted percentages.

The Vest results found that earnings from the multi-asset portfolio for the years 1968–1987 had nearly a 3.8 percent greater return versus that earned by the S&P 500 over the same time frame. More importantly, the average annual returns of the Vest portfolio comprised of multiple asset classifications achieved a lower risk level than America's best "Blue Chip" companies as represented by the S&P 500 benchmark.

The H.D. Vest Financial Services asset allocation study clearly illustrated how different types of assets perform under varying economic conditions, and the wisdom of instituting an asset allocation strategy in reducing risk and improving overall performance.

Multiple-asset portfolios work to reduce investors' exposure to risk for this reason: in different economic climates, the positive performance of one or more classes will overshadow any negative impact of underperforming categories within the same portfolio.

The combination of categories reduces the extreme reaction of any single category to varying economic scenarios. Consequently, over the long-term, the multi-asset portfolio lowers total portfolio risk without giving up long-term investment performance.

Figure 1–9, Asset Category Performance Under Different Economic Scenarios from H. D. Vest Financial Services chairman Herb D. Vest's book co-authored with Lynn Niedermeier, *Wealth: How to Get It, How to Keep It—the H.D. Vest System for Achieving Financial Security* (AMACOM, 1993), reflects how different asset categories have fared during consecutive periods of growth, inflation, and recession.

"In theory, the S&P 500 is determined to be the most diverse and best portfolio since it is a cross section of U.S. industry. However, in reality, it takes the narrow view that U. S. equities form the optimum portfolio mix. Extensive research has shown otherwise. Our studies use asset allocation with multi-asset categories

Figure 1–9
ASSET CATEGORY PERFORMANCE UNDER
DIFFERENT ECONOMIC SCENARIOS

Asset Category	Growth	Inflation	Recession
Large cap equities	Excellent	Poor	Excellent
Small cap equities	Excellent	Excellent	Excellent
Fixed income	Excellent	Poor	Good
International	Excellent	Excellent	Poor
Precious metals	Poor	Excellent	Excellent
Real estate	Excellent	Excellent	Excellent
Energy	Excellent	Good	Poor

Source: Vest & Niedermeier, "Wealth: How to Get It, How to Keep It" (Amacom, 1993).

to derive the optimum portfolio mix and reduce investor risk," says Vest.

According to Vest, you must consider three major factors when determining your investment strategy: return, risk, and the correlation between different asset classes. Once you have constructed your ideal portfolio mix, taking into consideration your risk tolerance and investment objectives, you must perform periodic rebalancing to keep your risk parameters intact.

For example, assume you start out with a mix of five categories with 20 percent invested in each. At the end of a given period the equity percentage has risen to 40 percent of the portfolio due to a dramatic rise in stock prices. Vest recommends rebalancing your portfolio to bring it back into the normal range. In other words, selling off equities and purchasing other investment categories to bring the mix back to desired proportions and risk levels.

"The specific combination of categories that is right for you depends on your investment goals, risk tolerance and time frame. Regardless of the mix of assets in the portfolio, however, the underlying concept is that the investments should work in harmony, with the various components performing differently under varying economic conditions. It is important that you optimize your "risk/reward ratio" through the careful selection of an investment portfolio. You can virtually eliminate risk higher than your tolerance level with the proper allocation," says Vest.

According to Vest, you can construct your own multi-asset portfolio in three easy steps. First, determine your financial objective either as a yearly percentage of return or the desired wealth to be accumulated after a period of years. Second, decide the level of risk you are truly comfortable taking on to achieve your investment objective. In other words, how much are you willing to lose in any given year given your long-term expected rate of return? Third, establish how long you are willing to wait to accomplish your goals.

Now you and/or your investment professional can match your financial profile with the appropriate mixture and proportions of various asset classifications to set your plan in action. This could involve investments in equities, fixed income instruments, international securities, precious metals, real estate, and energy.

In addition to constructing your own asset allocation portfolio, with or without a financial consultant's or broker's help, you can opt for the mutual fund alternative, seeking out allocation funds which take care of the professional money management and proper distribution and rebalancing of the portfolio.

Asset allocation funds may allow more leeway in their investing ranges, switching from 100 percent equities to 100 percent bonds depending on the economic environment. The strategy is catching on among investors. Through the first 11 months of 1992, these allocation funds attracted over $3 billion (net of redemptions and reinvested dividends). That's more than an eight-fold increase over the comparable prior year figure. Overall, the funds manage in excess of $14 billion.

The big drawback of many of these funds is that they don't invest in the wider spectrum of asset categories, sticking mainly to equities, bonds, and money market instruments.

Following is a partial list of asset allocation funds, complete with toll-free telephone numbers:

FUND	800 NUMBER
Fidelity Asset Manager	800-544-8888
Fidelity Asset Manager: Growth	800-544-8888
Merriman Asset Allocation	800-423-4893
Paine Webber Asset Allocation: A	800-647-1568
Paine Webber Asset Allocation: B	800-647-1568
Paine Webber Asset Allocation: D	800-647-1568
Permanent Portfolio	800-531-5142
Vanguard Asset Allocation	800-662-7447

Without a doubt, it makes sense to diversify your portfolio to reduce risk and enhance overall performance. Divide and conquer.

2

american depositary receipts and other global investing options

AMERICAN AND GLOBAL DEPOSITARY RECEIPTS

When you hear mention of ADRs, don't look for alien cousins of the adorable ALF. While ADRs do represent something foreign, they refer to ownership interests in foreign securities and not extra-terrestrial beings. However, savvy investing in ADRs can deliver out-of-this world investment returns and help protect your portfolio from risk through global diversification.

ADRs, American Depositary Receipts, originated way back in 1927 with Morgan Guaranty. Simply put, they are negotiable receipts held in a United States depositary bank, priced in dollars, for shares of a foreign company.

The beauty of ADRs is that they eliminate the need to understand the complexities of purchasing shares on foreign stock exchanges. ADRs make purchasing interests in foreign firms as easy as purchasing shares of domestic companies. All you need to do is call your broker and instruct him or her to purchase X number of shares (ADRs) at a certain price or at market.

ADRs also deliver another important feature. They increase the ease of geographically diversifying your investment portfolio, an important investing concept as we saw in Chapter One, "The Importance of Diversification Techniques."

According to the Bank of New York, which accounted for almost two-thirds of the new ADR issues brought to the market in recent years, there's a wealth of available ADRs from which to choose. ADR programs have surged to 924 at the end of 1992, up from only 683 in 1985. In fact, within the past five years, ADR trading volume grew approximately four times as fast as domestic equities.

The hot pace continued into 1993, with a record number of ADRs traded on U.S. exchanges during the first half of 1993. ADR trading increased 23 percent in number of shares and 28 percent in dollar value traded during the first half of 1993 compared with the first six months of 1992. By year end, 990 ADR programs were anticipated with a record 105 new programs in 1993.

"The increase in ADR volume indicates the growing interest among U.S. investors for international equities," said Joseph M. Velli, executive vice president in charge of The Bank of New York's Corporate Trust and Agency Services.

The United Kingdom accounts for 22 percent of all ADRs but you can purchase ADRs of companies from a wide variety of countries around the world including France, Italy, Japan, Mexico, The Netherlands, Norway, Spain, and Sweden. During 1992, nearly $125 billion in ADRs were traded on U.S. stock exchanges, over a 25 percent increase over 1991 ADR trading levels.

For the first time, companies from such countries as India (Reliance Industries), Taiwan (China Steel Corporation), and Brazil (Aracruz Celulose) established depositary receipt programs to raise capital in the United States.

"We anticipate seeing 15–20 new ADR programs from China in the next two years. In addition, Latin America is strong and privatization of French companies will result in more French ADR programs," said Velli.

ADRs also offer diversification by type of industry. You can choose from mining companies to utilities and from consumer goods firms to industrial product manufacturers. Illustrating the breadth of industries and geographical diversity available in the ADR realm, the foreign companies listed in Table 2–1 issued ADRs in the United States during 1992, and early 1993.

Table 2–1
ADR'S ISSUED IN THE UNITED STATES BY FOREIGN COMPANIES DURING 1992 AND EARLY 1993

Company	Country	Industry
Aracruz Celulose	Brazil	Pulp and paper
Asia Cement	Taiwan	Cement
Australian Con Press	Australia	Magazine publisher
BAESA	Argentina	Pepsi bottling
Dresdner Bank	Germany	Financial institution
Empresas	Mexico	Construction
Grand Hotel Hold Ltd	Hong Kong	Hotels
Lion Land Berhad	Malaysia	Holding company
Medeva plc	United Kingdom	Pharmaceutical
Reliance Industries	India	Conglomerate
Roche Holding	Switzerland	Drug/healthcare
Shiseido Co. Ltd.	Japan	Cosmetics
Telebras	Brazil	Telecommunications
Teva Pharmaceutical	Israel	Pharmaceutical
Venepal/Venprecar	Venezuela	Pulp and paper
Wellcome plc	United Kingdom	Pharmaceutical

According to the Bank of New York ADR statistics, non-U.S. companies raised a record $9.4 billion in equity capital in the U.S. in 1992, up 36 percent from 1991's record year of $6.9 billion.

Testifying to the growing importance of ADRs in the U.S. securities market, for the first time ever, a non-U.S. company, Glaxo Holdings PLC (the United Kingdom's largest drug company) ranked as the most actively traded equity in the United States with a trading volume of over 569 million shares worth over $15.7 billion.

The largest dollar volume in ADRs during 1992, however, goes to Telefonos de Mexico Series L (Mexican telecommunications company) with over $23.3 billion traded on the New York Stock Exchange involving 464.9 million shares. Other leading ADR companies in 1992 in terms of shares or dollar volume traded are shown in Table 2–2.

Table 2–2
ADR COMPANIES

Company	Country	Share Volume	Dollar Volume
Hanson plc	U.K.	184,922,300	$ 3.5 Billion
Royal Dutch	Netherlands	184,487,400	15.6 Billion
British Pet	U.K.	174,182,200	8.8 Billion
Tele de Espana	Spain	92,763,800	3.0 Billion
Wellcome plc	U.K.	90,092,700	1.4 Billion
SmithKline Bee	U.K.	80,233,600	4.2 Billion
Reuters Hold	U.K.	72,165,800	4.4 Billion
Ericsson Tel	Sweden	70,536,800	1.6 Billion
Unilever	Netherlands	59,504,600	6.2 Billion
News Corp	Australia	57,026,700	1.9 Billion

Overall, ADR trading on U.S. exchanges (NYSE, AMEX, and NASDAQ) in 1992 totaled 4.3 billion Depositary Receipts valued at approximately $125 billion, a 33 percent dollar volume increase over 1991 levels.

Figure 2–1, Total Number of Depositary Receipt Programs, Figure 2–2, Percentage of Total Depositary Receipt Programs by Country, and Figure 2–3, Depositary Receipt Dollar Trading Vol-

Figure 2–1
TOTAL NUMBER OF DEPOSITARY RECEIPT PROGRAMS
January 1, 1993 through June 30, 1993

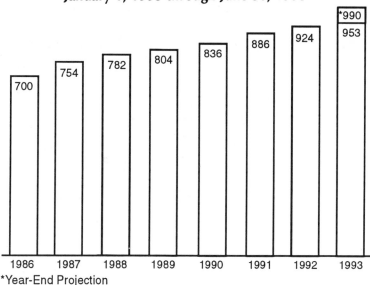

*Year-End Projection

Source: The Bank of New York.

ume by Country reflect the wide variety of ADRs to choose from in globally diversifying your portfolio.

Currently, less than five percent of U.S. equity investments are overseas, but the trend is growing toward greater participation by American money in foreign securities.

"I foresee overseas investing approaching 15–20 percent by the end of the decade," says Mark Coler, president of Mercer, Inc., a New York City-based research company that specializes in following activity in the ADR market and publishes *The Global Portfolio*.

There are two types of ADRs, sponsored and unsponsored. Sponsored ADRs comply with all the disclosure and reporting requirements of the Securities and Exchange Commission, just like their U.S. company counterparts. Unsponsored ADRs, on the other hand, are created by a bank to satisfy investor demand for a

Figure 2–2
PERCENTAGE OF TOTAL DEPOSITARY
RECEIPT PROGRAMS BY COUNTRY
January 1, 1993 through June 30, 1993

As of June 30, 1993 there were 953 Depositary Receipt Programs

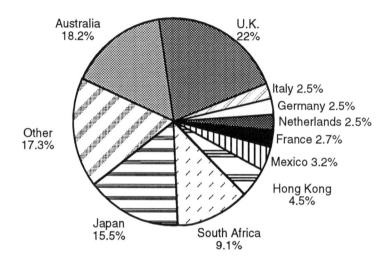

Source: The Bank of New York.

foreign security, and registered with the SEC but do not have to comply with all the financial reporting requirements.

An unsponsored ADR does not mean it's an indication of a bad investment, but it may be harder to obtain financial information to evaluate and compare an unsponsored ADR with other investment alternatives. For instance, your annual report may be printed in Spanish and denominated in pesos rather than in English and U.S. dollars.

ADRs offer a number of important advantages over purchasing foreign securities on foreign exchanges. First of all, you avoid the complexities of foreign exchange trading rules. Second, ADR

Figure 2–3
DEPOSITARY RECEIPT DOLLAR TRADING
VOLUME BY COUNTRY
January 1, 1993 through June 30, 1993

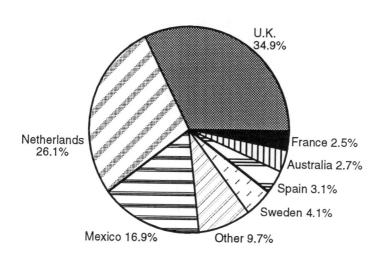

Source: The Bank of New York.

delivery typically takes only a few days versus several weeks or even months in the case of foreign equities. Third, price quotes are more readily available. Fourth, as mentioned earlier many ADR companies provide more complete financial information and the reports are printed in English. Fifth, ADRs are insured by SIPC, which prevents the investor from getting burned in the event of their brokerage firm failure.

There are a few minor drawbacks to ADR investing. The bank may charge a small service fee for handling cash dividend conversions to dollars from the native currency. As with any foreign investment, there's also the risk of currency translation losses as the U.S. dollar and the foreign currency fluctuate in relation to each other with changing international economic environments.

Another inconvenience, some ADRs trade on the pink sheets with relatively low volume, resulting in thin liquidity. However, just because an ADR is traded on the pink sheets does not mean it's a small company. Such corporate giants as Mitsubishi Corporation (Japan) and Nestle S.A. (Switzerland) trade on the pink sheets despite their international renown and heavy trading volumes.

Likewise, companies with unsponsored ADRs should not be snubbed either. Many leading international companies such as The Netherlands' The Unilever Group and Japan's Toyota Motor Corporation entered the U.S. securities markets as unsponsored ADRs.

With all that in mind, where do you find opportunities for ADR investing?

Mexico's torrid market has resulted in the ADRs of Mexican companies becoming one of the ADR hot spots in both 1991 and 1992. In response to investor demand, the number of Mexican ADRs traded on U.S. exchanges jumped from only three in July 1989 to more than 30 in 1993.

One Mexican ADR that sold faster than hot tamales at a bullfight, Telefonos de Mexico (TELMEX), more than doubled its early 1991 price to over $60 per share before drifting to around $47 1/2 per share in mid-1993. TELMEX stands to benefit from Mexico's improving economic situation and increased demand since only approximately six percent of the Mexican population is now served by phone service.

Kathleen Updike, a grade school teacher from Palatine, Illinois, knows the lure and profit possibilities of investing in Mexican companies. Back in 1983, Updike purchased shares of Telmex for just over $1 per share. Later, in 1986, she upped her stake in the Mexican telecommunications giant when its stock price dropped to 5/32. To make a long story short, Updike transformed her original $500 Telmex investment into over $16,000, not a bad return on her money. Updike did hear about Telmex from her broker.

In 1992, I wrote an article on Mexican investments that appeared as a feature in the April 1992 issue of *Kiplinger's Personal Finance Magazine*. While the torrid pace of the Mexican market has tempered somewhat since then, a number of key fundamentals remain in place that could heat up Mexican stocks once again.

Following a 43 percent jump in Mexico's leading stock index in 1990, the index surged another 126 percent in 1991 and jumped even higher to reach a peak of 1907 in June 1992. In mid-1993, the Mexican Bolsa stood at 1672.

The North American Free Trade Agreement (NAFTA) has been temporarily derailed, but most political and economic pundits agree that it will be back on track again. The economic benefits on both sides of the border could be a major boon for many well-positioned Mexican companies.

Other economic positives bode well for Mexico's economic future and its companies' fortunes. Mexico's taming of its inflation rate, down from 157 percent in 1987 to 11.9 percent for 1992, adds stability to the country's economic policies and the international competitiveness of Mexican companies.

In addition, reduction of Mexico's national debt works to streamline the economy and decrease debt service. Continued privatization of state-owned businesses and increased foreign investment in Mexico promise to increase efficiency and provide the capital for expanded business opportunities.

Of course, risks do exist when investing in any foreign company. NAFTA could be derailed permanently, inflation could rear its ugly head once again, debt levels could rise if government programs get too ambitious or don't work out as well as planned, and political battles could sink some of the progressive reforms which have been put into action or delay other planned economic reforms.

"At 11 times estimated 1993 earnings and 2.2 times book value, the Mexican market looks reasonably priced for a fast growing economy, especially when compared to the U.S. market," says Coler.

According to *The Global Portfolio*, the Mexican Bolsa is the largest and most liquid in Latin America with a market capitalization of $133 billion as of January 1993. Among emerging markets, Mexico is exceeded in market capitalization only by Hong Kong.

Two Mexican companies reviewed by *The Global Portfolio*, CIFRA and CEMEX, offer investors some interesting prospects.

CIFRA ranks as the Mexican Walmart, the largest and most efficient retailer in Mexico. In fact, CIFRA has inked a joint venture agreement with U.S.-based Walmart, which promises to turn CIFRA into a world-class company in the not-too distant future. To be sure, CIFRA will encounter stiff competition for market share but should be able to deliver earnings gains approaching 20 percent in 1993 and over the near term.

A word of caution, however. In early 1993, CIFRA traded over $2.00 per share, about 30 times price earnings and approximately two times the average price earnings ratio for the Mexican market.

CEMEX leads Mexican cement producers with 63 percent of the Mexican cement market and 72 percent of domestic ready mix. Negative institutional investor reaction to the company's $1.8 billion bid for Spain's two largest cement companies sank the stock like one of the firm's own cement blocks. The ADRs fell below $25 per share from the $40 per share level in early 1992.

Contrarian investors looked at CEMEX's solid fundamentals such as high margins, its position as one of the world's low cost producers, and extremely favorable revenue potential based on the Mexican's government's top priority on building the country's infrastructure, and bought in. The moved paid off as CEMEX's price recovered to the $32 per share level.

It pays to study the market, company, and industry fundamentals to take advantage of special situations or investor overreactions.

"The fact that the Mexican market has attracted so much investor attention over the past two years increases the risk that the market may become overbought," warns Coler.

Other foreign investment opportunities exist in the European arena and Far East. As the European community comes together and the current economic recession disappears, European companies can tap new market opportunities. Table 2–3, Strong European Market Performance, shows European stock markets which exhibited good performance during the first six months of 1993.

Table 2–3
STRONG EUROPEAN MARKET PERFORMANCE
FIRST SIX MONTHS OF 1993

Country	6/30/93 Market Close	YTD % Change
Spain	259.8	21.3%
Italy	1183.0	19.7
Netherlands	228.9	15.6
Belgium	1279.5	13.5
Germany	1697.6	9.9
France	1971.9	6.1

Likewise, Pacific Rim countries possess the resources and opportunity to resume robust growth with an upturn in the global economy.

ADR information sources, in addition to your broker, include *The Global Portfolio* published by Mercer, Inc., *The International Company Handbook* distributed by Gateway Lake Headquarters in Pompano Beach, Florida, and Standard & Poor's *The Outlook*.

ADRs represent a unique way for the U.S. investor to benefit from global diversification while avoiding the hassle of purchasing stock on foreign exchanges.

GLOBAL DEPOSITARY RECEIPTS, ETC.

A discussion of a new player, Global Depositary Receipts, is in order. While ADRs have been on the scene for nearly 70 years, only in recent years have individual investors taken notice of their ease of use and numerous benefits. Now, with the recent explosion of global securities, the use of depositary receipts has extended beyond the United States.

In a number of global offerings in the last few years, the terms Global Depositary Receipts (GDRs), International Depositary Receipts (IDRs), and European Depositary Receipts (EDRs) have come into use. The fundamental relationship between the underlying security and the depositary receipt remains the same, as does the degree of service offered by the depositary bank. In order to eliminate confusion, some professionals in the depositary receipt field have recommended that the term Depositary Receipt (DR) be adopted for all such receipts having the characteristics of the ADR.

The Mutual and Country Fund Options

Of course, you can leave the individual foreign stock picking to professional money managers and invest in one or more of the many single country, region, global, or international mutual funds which have proliferated during the past decade.

Mutual fund investors who shifted assets to international funds during the first four and a half months of 1993 saw their portfolios outperform their U.S. counterparts substantially.

According to Lipper Analytical Services, during that time frame international mutual funds earned 13.7 percent versus only around three percent for U.S. mutual funds. Contributing to the better international performance are the relatively high multiples commanded by U.S. stocks as the Dow Jones Industrial Average continued to trend into higher territory and more vibrant economies outside of the United States as it still struggled with a lingering recession in 1993.

Table 2–4 provides a representative sampling of top 1992 mutual funds operating in the foreign, global and international arenas.

Table 2–4
TOP 1992 MUTUAL FUNDS OPERATING IN THE FOREIGN,
GLOBAL, AND INTERNATIONAL ARENAS

Fund	Fund Type	Telephone Number	One Year (92) Performance
Fidelity Int Op	International	800-544-8888	+5.9%
59 Wall St Eur	Europe	212-493-8100	+7.5%
Janus Worldwide	Global	800-525-3713	+9.0%
Keystone Am Gl	Global Sml Co	800-343-2898	+11.4%
Morgan Stanley	Pacific Region	800-548-7786	+26.4%
Merrill L.A. A	Latin America	800-637-3863	+2.2%

Morgan Stanley Asian Equity Fund targets investing at least 65 percent of its assets in the common stocks of Asian issuers whose countries have the more established markets in the region. It uses a value approach to investing in large companies or small to medium companies with growth potential.

Past performance is no guarantee of future results. Evaluate each fund in relation to current and projected economic trends and holdings.

International and global equity funds have attracted strong investor interest. Since 1984, the number of such funds has increased more than ten-fold, from 21 to over 250 international and global equity funds.

According to the Investment Company Institute, over the past nine years, total assets in international and global equity funds surged from $4.3 billion to nearly $51.6 billion.

The United States's share of world market value of equities continues to shrink. In 1971, the U.S. accounted for over 68 percent of world equity market value. Twenty years later, that share decreased to around 38 percent. It only makes good investing sense to diversify your portfolio into the international and global markets, expanding your investment options and profit possibilities.

Overseas equity market performance has also outperformed that of the U.S. market for the decade 1982–1992. According to

Morgan Stanley Capital International data, the U.S. market ranked 13th with a 16.0 percent return. Taking top honors was the Hong Kong equity market with a 25.5 percent return. The top ten performers are listed in Table 2–5, Top World Equity Markets, 1982–1992.

Table 2–5
TOP TEN WORLD EQUITY MARKETS
ANNUALIZED TOTAL RETURNS 1982–1992

Rank	Market	% Return*
1.	Hong Kong	25.5%
2.	Belgium	25.4
3.	France	23.1
4.	The Netherlands	22.1
5.	Spain	20.9
6.	Austria	20.3
7.	United Kingdom	19.9
8.	Sweden	17.6
9.	Switzerland	17.0
10.	Norway	16.5

* In U.S. Dollars

Overseas investing is not just limited to stocks. Numerous international and global fixed income funds strive to deliver higher returns via global diversification. According to Salomon Brothers statistics, foreign bonds account for 66 percent of the value of the world's bond markets versus only 34 percent for U.S. bonds. That compares with the 51 percent share of world bond value U.S. bonds garnered as recently as 1980.

Salomon Brothers data also reflects that for the period from 1984 through 1992, U.S. government bonds earned an average annual return of 11.3 percent versus 19.3 percent, 17.1 percent, 16.6

percent, and 16.5 percent for France, The Netherlands, Japan, and Germany, respectively.

Closed-end country funds represent another opportunity for investors to participate in the international markets.

"The U.S. markets have underperformed many overseas markets in recent years. Growth rates for many other countries are strong, translating to better percentage gains than available in the U.S. For example, during the first half of 1993, the Dow gained around 6.5 percent while the Turkish Investment Fund jumped over 90 percent in net asset value (NAV) and over 73 percent in price change," says Thomas J. Herzfeld, president of Thomas J. Herzfeld Advisors, Inc. in Miami, Florida and author of *Herzfeld's Guide to Closed-End Funds* (McGraw-Hill, 1993).

Table 2–6 shows the top ten performing foreign equity funds during the first half of 1993 in terms of percent price change.

Table 2–6
TOP TEN EQUITY FUNDS
FIRST HALF OF 1993
BY PERCENT PRICE CHANGE

Foreign Equity Fund		% Price Change
1.	Turkish Investment Fund	73.8%
2.	Japan Equity Fund	52.9
3.	Singapore Fund	49.4
4.	Brazilian Equity Fund	44.4
5.	Templeton Emerging Markets	39.1
6.	Italy Fund	35.0
7.	Scudder New Asia Fund	31.3
8.	The China Fund	29.8
9.	Jardine Fleming China Reg. Fund	29.1
10.	First Phillipine Fund	26.8

Remember, current performance is no indication of future performance. For example, in 1990 (a bad year for country funds) Turkish Investment Fund declined over 43 percent in price, then went on to gain 16.5 percent in 1991 and lose 30.6 percent in 1992 before moving ahead again during the first half of 1993.

Templeton Emerging Growth declined 1.61 percent in price in 1990, gained 98.1 percent in 1991, lost 8.9 percent in 1992, and posted a price gain of 39.1 percent for the first half of 1993.

Obviously, investors in closed-end country funds can be in for some pretty volatile rides. You have to have the investment temperament to withstand wide swings in both NAV and fund prices.

"There are plenty of opportunities in country funds, but there are also risks such as political, currency, lack of regulation, and different accounting standards for foreign companies, which have to be assessed against the tremendous potential gains," advises Herzfeld.

On the plus side: country funds are easy to invest in, meet New York Stock Exchange listing requirements, have ample liquidity, and are run by professional money managers well-versed in the economics and politics of the countries of the companies in which they invest.

In September 1990, Herzfeld launched a program to invest in country funds. The program is managed by his advisory firm and required an initial investment of $100,000 per unit. As of June 30, 1993, one unit's value totaled $176,600. Herzfeld's single country fund program still takes new investors but they must match the current unit value, $176,600 as of June 1993.

Herzfeld sees Cuba as one of the promising country funds of the future. In fact, in August, 1993, his firm formed a new unit, Herzfeld-Cuba, to direct investments throughout the Caribbean Basin. He planned to underwrite and manage The Herzfeld Caribbean Basin Fund (the SEC will not allow Herzfeld to use "Cuba" in the fund's name) to capitalize on the tremendous growth potential of Cuba after it casts aside the aging Fidel Castro.

Herzfeld also publishes a research report entitled *The Investor's Guide to Closed-End Funds* on a monthly basis. The annual subscription rate is $325 or a two-month trial subscription runs $60. A free sample copy is available upon request. You can order from Thomas J. Herzfeld Advisors, Inc., P. O. Box 161465, Miami, Florida 33116 or call 305-271-1900.

Morningstar publishes *Morningstar Closed-End Funds*. An annual subscription costs $195 and a three-month trial goes for $35. Order from Morningstar, 53 W. Jackson Boulevard, Chicago, IL 60604, or call 800-876-5005.

Another source of closed-end fund information and buy/sell/hold recommendations derives from *The Scott Letter: Closed-End Fund Report* published by George Cole Scott, and co-author of *Investing in Closed-End Funds: Finding Value and Building Wealth* (New York Institute of Finance, 1991). An annual subscription costs $135 and can be ordered from *The Scott Letter*, Box 17800, Richmond, Virginia 23226 or call 1-800-356-3508.

The Scott Letter also contains an equity portfolio. A recent addition to the portfolio as of August 1993, the Swiss Helvetia Fund invests in equity and debt of blue chip Swiss companies such as Nestle. The fund originally issued shares in July 1988 at $12 per share and traded at a nearly five percent discount to NAV in mid-1993 with a price of $16 1/4 per share. Swiss Helvetia Fund earned a total return of 7.5 percent in 1992.

One of the top performing country funds in *The Scott Letter* portfolio in 1992, The First Philippine Fund earned a 1992 total return of 23.49 percent. The fund invests 80 percent in Philippine equities and delivered a compound annual return of 11.9 percent from inception in November 1989 to March 31, 1993.

Due to the unique nature of closed-end funds and the differences that arise between their NAVs and market prices, a further discussion of closed-end funds is in order.

First of all, closed-end funds, unlike their open-ended mutual fund counterparts, have a limited number of shares outstanding. Upon inception, they issue a fixed number of shares and trade on a securities exchange just like any stock. While open-end mutual funds trade at NAV, closed-end funds have both an NAV and current market price which fluctuates depending on the fund's prospects (the performance of the individual securities held) and market sentiment.

Since underwriting spreads on new issue closed-end funds can run as high as eight percent, it's wise to avoid new funds and concentrate on funds after the underwriting premium has been absorbed and the fund starts trading on it own merits. Track the fund's performance in relation to investment objectives detailed in the prospectus.

One of the advantages of the closed-end fund stems from the fund management's ability to fully utilize investment monies since it does not have to maintain large cash reserves for anticipated share redemptions as in open-end funds. The capital can be put to use generating higher returns for investors.

Closed-end funds can be used to target specialized investment niches such as single country, industry, convertible securities, and foreign government bonds.

Often, closed-end funds trade at a discount to NAV. For example, a fund with a NAV of $10 per share might trade at a 10 percent discount or market price of $9 per share, meaning you get $10 in assets for every $9 invested. A discounted fund typically offers a degree of down-side protection. As the NAV declines, the share price often declines less proportionally.

To illustrate, during a market decline, the NAV might fall 20 percent from $10 to $8 per share while the fund's market discount may actually narrow. In this case, the share price might drop to $7.20 from $8 per share, only a 10 percent decline. Of course, such a price movement is not guaranteed and you run the risk that the NAV drop may be compounded by a widening of the discount.

Track the fund's historical discount from NAV and search out opportunities to purchase oversold closed-end funds whose fundamentals remain attractive.

No matter which way you decide to participate in global investment opportunities, you owe it to yourself to investigate the wealth of options and choose the one or ones which match your investment goals and risk posture best.

3

captivating
convertibles

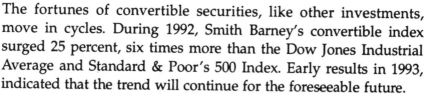

The fortunes of convertible securities, like other investments, move in cycles. During 1992, Smith Barney's convertible index surged 25 percent, six times more than the Dow Jones Industrial Average and Standard & Poor's 500 Index. Early results in 1993, indicated that the trend will continue for the foreseeable future.

According to Moody's Investors Service, $9.32 billion in convertible securities were issued in 1992 on top of $16.39 billion in 1991 from $10.8 billion in 1990. For the first half of 1993, $5.0 billion in convertible securities hit the streets. Not all of these new convertibles will be available to the general investing public directly. A number of issues are sold as private placements to institutional investors and the individual investor can participate in these new convertible issues through mutual funds specializing in convertibles.

Just what are convertible securities and why should the individual investor consider them as a part of his or her investment portfolio strategy?

Many investors risk losing out on unique investment opportunities because they do not understand convertible terminology and the basics of convertible investing. It's not very complicated and a few minutes of your time taken to understand and evaluate convertibles can pay off big, especially when other traditional investments look less than attractive due to the current interest rate environment, yields, and stock market action.

Simply put, the convertible represents a hybrid security with the attributes of both equities and fixed income instruments. The purchaser of a convertible security obtains the right to exchange the security for a specified number of shares of the underlying company's common stock, thus the name "convertible."

This privilege allows the convertible owner to participate in the upside potential of the common stock since it can be converted into common stock. In addition, the convertible earns a stated dividend (in the case of convertible preferred stock) and interest rate (in the case of convertible bonds), giving it attributes of a fixed income security.

Therefore, as the price of the underlying common stock rises, the convertible's market price tends to track that movement. Prices of convertibles typically rise slower than the common stock until the stock price rises above the conversion price (the conversion price is the common stock price at which the convertible holder breaks even on the conversion). After that point, the convertible's upside potential closely correlates with common stock price movements.

Conversely, as the price of the underlying common stock drifts lower, the convertible's market price tends to drift lower at a slower rate. This occurs because the fixed income attributes of the convertible kick in and support the convertible's price level. Its trading action now moves more like a straight bond due to its interest paying ability and since its convertibility function has become less valuable as the common stock price drops far below the conversion price.

In other words, the convertible investor gets the best of both worlds: participation in upside moves of the underlying common stock and protection on the downside when the fixed income protection comes into play.

Savvy investors wary of volatile markets can lock in an attractive yield and still maintain the ability to earn capital gains if the stock market and stock price of the underlying stock turn up. The convertible's hybrid attributes enable the investor to earn a yield higher than that obtainable by owning the common stock, to participate in appreciation of the common stock price, and to gain protection against downside pressures of stock market moves.

There's another important reason to consider convertible investing. Since convertibles occupy a senior position in relation to common stock, convertible holders always receive their dividend or interest payments prior to common stock owners. In addition, they also possess a superior claim on company assets in the event of a bankruptcy or liquidation.

Companies like to issue convertible securities for several reasons. First of all, convertibles typically carry a lower coupon or dividend rate than straight bonds or preferred stock. Second, they normally sell at a premium due to the convertibility provision. Finally, since investors can only economically convert into stock after the shares trade at higher than the issuance price, issuers are guaranteed that any new stock issue will later be sold at a higher price, thus garnering more capital for company coffers.

There's been criticism of convertibles in the past that most covertible offerings originate from small, less financially secure companies with an inactive aftermarket. This is certainly less true today when companies such as American Brands, Baxter International, Ford Motor, Hecla Mining, Home Depot, and Ogden Corporation are issuing convertible securities.

Firms offering convertibles run the gamut from the bluest of "Blue Chip" firms to new companies. Like any other investment, it pays to investigate the financial stability and track record of the firm and top management. *Barron's, Investor's Business Daily,* and *The Wall Street Journal* as well as many major daily newspapers, carry listings of convertible securities. Look for a separate convertible classification or the symbol "cv" to determine available issues in which you can invest.

LEARNING THE TERMS

The first step in learning how to navigate convertible waters begins with learning their unique terminology. A review of the following terms and definitions will provide you the knowledge required to decipher the world of convertible investing.

■ **Busted Convertible:** A convertible that trades only on the basis of its yield, similar to a straight bond, since its stock price trades far below the conversion price.

■ **Call provision:** The right of the issuer to redeem the convertible bond before maturity under certain conditions.

■ **Call protection:** Built in covenants prohibiting or restricting the issuer from redeeming the convertible.

■ **Conversion equivalent:** The adjusted price at which the stock must sell to be of equal value with the convertible security. The following formula illustrates how to calculate the converison equivalent:

$$\text{Conversion Equivalent} = \frac{\text{Market Price of Bond}}{\text{Number of Shares Received}}$$

■ **Conversion premium:** The difference in value between the convertible's selling price and its conversion value. The conversion premium changes in relation to various factors such as yield advantage over the underlying common stock, common stock price movements, changes in perception of the underlying company's economic fortunes, actual company financial and operational results, and interpretations of how well the convertible will track changes in the common stock price.

■ **Conversion price:** The common stock price at which the security may be converted.

- **Conversion rate:** The number of shares of common stock which the convertible holder receives in the conversion for each $1,000 convertible bond or share of preferred convertible stock. To determine the number of shares allowable in a conversion, divide the $1,000 par value by the conversion price. In other words, a convertible bond exchangeable into common stock at $25 per share will convert to 40 shares of common stock (1,000/25).

- **Conversion value:** The current value of the convertible if converted to stock. Calculated by multiplying the number of shares of stock to be received (conversion rate) times the current common stock market price.

- **Convertible preferred stock:** Shares of preferred stock convertible into shares of common stock. See Chapter 7, Preferreds.

- **Convertible zero-coupon bonds:** Zero coupon bonds convertible into shares of common stock. See Chapter 10, Zeroing in on Zeros.

- **Coupon:** The stated interest rate on a bond. The current yield could be more or less depending on the market price.

- **Investment (floor) value:** The value of the bond if it traded as a straight bond without benefit of the convertibility provision.

A convertible bond selling at 102 and exchangeable for 25 shares of XYZ Corporation common stock has a conversion value of $40.80 (1020/25). Assume XYZ's common stock currently sells for $46 per share. In that case, the shareholder should convert and earn a profit of $5.20 ($46.00–$40.80) per share. If XYZ common stock sells for less than $40.80 per share, it makes no sense to convert so the investor would continue to hold the security and earn the fixed rate of interest while waiting for the stock market price to rise above the conversion price.

In reality, most investors don't go through the conversion process, since the stock of the convertible tends to track the change in common stock price. However, the market is not perfect and anomalies do exist.

There are a number of factors which must be considered before investing in convertible securities. As in any investment, it's crucial to investigate the soundness of the issuing corporation, including the prospects for both short and long-term earnings growth. A review of industry conditions is also in order. Ask yourself, what technological, competitive, economic, etc., changes could negatively impact the company and its industry?

An evaluation of prior price action of the underlying common stock also needs to be addressed. If the conversion price is $40 per share and the company's common stock price has never surpassed $30 per share, the likelihood of a profitable conversion is called into serious question.

It also makes good sense to study the current interest rate environment in relation to the premium on a convertible security in order to properly evaluate and compare other investment alternatives.

Call provisions and call protection also come into play when assessing convertibles. The call provision gives the issuer the right to redeem or call the convertible before maturity. If the bonds are trading higher than the call price, the investor could stand to lose the difference between the convertible's market price and its call price. Even if the investor does not lose money based on the call price, he or she loses earnings potential based on the higher yield paid by the convertible over possible alternative investments.

Don't be caught unaware; check out the call provisions both as to call prices and call dates before you invest. At the same time, inquire about call protection, those provisions preventing or restricting when and how an issuer can call a convertible.

Along with the premium convertibles command, each convertible has a "break-even" or "payback period" associated with it. This is length of time it takes to repay, in interest, the amount paid over its conversion price. In other words, how long it takes to earn back the premium paid through interest earnings. A long payback period can make the security less desirable in comparison to other investments and the underlying common stock.

Evaluate what the investor obtains for the premium. Does he or she get a higher yield than that available on the underlying common stock as well as an opportunity to participate in the rise in price of the common stock?

Now, assume you purchase a convertible bond with a face value of $1,000 and that is exchangeable into common stock at $20 per share (in other words, convertible into 50 shares [1,000/20]), and pay $1,000 for the bond. Assume that this bond has a coupon rate of six percent and the common stock trades for $18 per share and yields two percent.

Currently, the value of the underlying common stock on the $1,000 bond is $900 (50 x $18). Since the bond was purchased for $1,000, you paid a $100 premium ($1,000 – $900) for the higher yield and chance to participate in higher common stock prices.

The bond earns $60 per year in interest while the stock pays cash dividends of two percent or $.36 per share annually. Common stock dividends on the 50 shares would total $18 per year. By purchasing the convertible bond you earn $42 more in interest per year ($60 – $18) for the same dollar investment. At this earnings difference, your premium payback period works out to around 2.4 years.

With many convertibles offering yields anywhere from four to eight percent, they represent an enticing alternative to low yielding stocks and even lower yielding money market funds.

The trick is to ferret out the convertibles (and underlying companies) that will hold value and rise in price with improved earnings and a better economy. If the economy takes longer to materialize, the convertible owner can sit tight with his or her higher yields.

In mid-1993, convertibles offered yields double that of common stocks and nearly equal or better than many utilities. In addition, they offered superior capital gains potential to a majority of utilities and could share in the upside moves of common stocks.

You don't have to wait until the common stock price pushes past the conversion price to make money on convertibles. Assume you purchase a $1,000 bond convertible into common stock at $40 per share (25 shares conversion rate). With the stock trading at $35 per share, it does not make sense to convert since the stock value only amounts to $875 ($35 x 25).

Now, if the stock price rises just over 14 percent to $40 per share, it still does not make sense to convert because the value of the stock now totals $1,000 ($40 x 25), or exactly what you paid for the bond. However, if the convertible bond tracked the 14 percent rise in common stock price but at a lower level, say a 10 percent rise in bond value, what would happen? This would create a bond market price of $1,100 per bond. You could now sell the bond for a capital gain of $100 (less transaction costs), not to mention the interest earned in the meantime.

As the common stock rises further above the conversion price, the convertible security will start to trade less and less like a bond and more and more like the common stock, narrowing the gap between the price of the bond and the market value of the underlying common stock.

"First and foremost in convertible investing, you must like the prospects of the underlying company and its stock or you don't invest in the convertible," says John Ferreby, senior investment manager for National Asset Management Corporation in Louisville, Kentucky.

Ferreby searches out convertibles which trade at very low premiums and offer a higher yield than that which can be earned by owning the company's common stock. Ferreby then reviews call provisions to ensure he can earn back that premium in the next few years and then earn a higher yield.

For example, Emerson Electric Company (NYSE: EMR) sports a long track record of increasing earnings per share as well as a rising stock price trendline from the early eighties through mid-1993. See Figure 3–1, Emerson Electric Company.

Figure 3–1
EMERSON ELECTRIC COMPANY

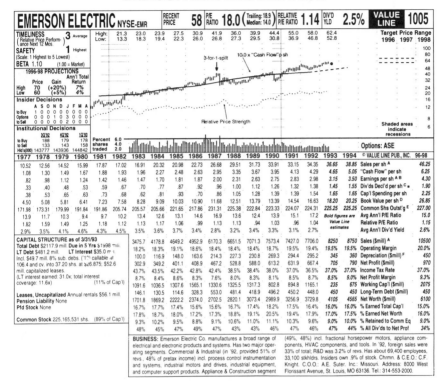

Source: Reprinted by permission. Copyright 1993, Value Line Publishing, Inc. All Rights reserved.

The St. Louis, Missouri electrical and electronic company stands to benefit from a rise in economic activity both in the U.S. and abroad. In addition, key acquisitions promise to make significant inroads in overseas markets while increased research and development expenses are paying off in new products.

To take advantage of the convertible edge, Ferreby sold 37,083 shares of Emerson Electric common stock in accounts managed by National Asset Management at $54.775 per share. At the same time, he purchased $1 million par value of Emerson Electric November 15, 2010 bonds convertible into 37.083 shares of common stock. The maneuver allowed Ferreby to earn an additional

$26,600 in interest annually over what he would have earned in dividends on the common stock. For this he paid a premium of $5,400, meaning that in less than one-third of a year, he would payback the premium paid for the convertible bonds.

While you may not have the $1 million-plus to invest in one transaction, the basic principal of convertible investing remains the same.

Illustrating the Principles

Sandra Shrewsbury, manager of Piper Jaffray's Emerging Growth Fund in Minneapolis, offers three scenarios for convertible investing with appropriate real company examples to illustrate the principles at work.

Example 1, Norwest Corporation (NYSE: NOB) You like the common stock yet would like to earn a higher yield. For example, Norwest Corporation resides in an industry group with good momentum. The nation's 14th largest bank holding company ranks as a premier superregional banking company. Norwest's service market includes the Upper Midwest and Rocky Mountain regions, both areas which have been less impacted by the recent recession than have other sections of the country. The company sports a great balance sheet, strong capital position, and excellent credit quality.

In other words, Norwest represents a solid stock position to add to your portfolio. But by holding the company's $3.50 convertible preferred, you can increase your yield from the 2.5 percent paid on the common stock to 4.5 percent on the preferred stock and still participate in the upside potential of the common stock.

The Norwest Corporation $3.50 convertible preferred (NYSE: NOB.B) is convertible into 2.742 shares of common stock yielding a conversion value of $72.32. The issue possesses call protection until September 1, 1995. The first call price starts at $52.10 per share and scales down to $50.00 per share in the year 2001. In early August 1993, at a convertible price of $78.50 price per share and a common price of $26.38 per share, the preferred has a premium of 8.5 percent and would require 4.01 years to breakeven.

Example 2, DNA Plant Technology (NASDAQ: DNAP) In this instance, you like the prospects of the company but it is early stage and pays no dividend. DNA Plant Technology, in all likelihood, won't generate any profits until 1996 and currently pays no dividends to help offset the investment risk of betting on the come.

The agricultural biotechnology firm has interesting prospects over the long-term with biotechnology products in branded produce, vegetable oils, and diagnostic kits for agricultural diseases. However, the payoff, if any, could be years away. Investment in DNA Plant Technology common stock would represent an aggressive investment stance which many investors may not wish to make.

On the other hand, while still aggressive, purchasing the $2.25 convertible preferred delivers an attractive nine percent yield making the wait more palatable and reducing the overall level of risk.

DNA Plant Technology's $2.25 convertible preferred (NASDAQ: DNAPP) converts into 4.065 shares of common stock at a conversion value of $19.31. First call date is August 2, 1994 with a first call price of $26.80 per share. In early August 1993, the convertible preferred price stood at $25.00 per share and the common stock price was $4.75 per share. This calculated out to a premium of 29.5 percent and a breakeven period of 2.53 years.

Example 3, Champion International Corporation (NYSE: CHA)
You realize the industry is currently out of favor but would like to establish a position to benefit when the economic cycle becomes more favorable for company prospects. Champion International Corporation serves the printing and writing paper, newsprint, and lumber markets. The company had declining earnings for the past several years but the future looks brighter if the economy picks up steam.

The key point here is that you cannot accurately pinpoint when the economy will rebound and Champion's common share price starts to rise.

So, instead of earning a measly .6 percent yield on Champion's common stock while you wait for the turnaround, you can earn 6.1 percent on the firm's $6.50 coupon convertible subordinated debenture.

Champion International's $6.50 coupon convertible subordinated bond (CHA/11) can be exchanged for 28.78 shares of common stock with a conversion value of $94.62. The bonds are callable at $101.95 until April 15, 1994. In early August with a bond price of $106 and common price of $32.88 per share, Champion International's convertible bond commanded a 12.0 percent premium and would take 1.94 years to breakeven.

In order to make the proper investment and risk analysis, it's important to determine both the premium and breakeven period.

To calculate the percentage premium you pay, divide the excess of the market value of the convertible over its conversion value. For example, in the Champion International example above the convertible has a conversion value of $946.19 and sells in the market at $1060.00 per bond. The conversion premium percentage calculates as follows:

$$[(\$1060.00-\$946.19)/\$946.19] =$$

$$\$113.81/\$946.19 = 12.0\%$$

Now, to determine how long it would take to earn back the 12.0 percent premium, you need to divide the premium amount by the difference between the two payouts. The bond earns $65.00 per year while the equivalent amount of stock earns $5.76 ($.20 x 28.78) per year. An easy approximation of the breakeven period calculates to:

$$[\$113.91/(\$65.00-\$5.76)] =$$

$$\$113.91/\$59.24 = 1.92 \text{ years}$$

Busted Convertibles

Another way to invest in convertibles is to seek "busted convertibles," securities whose underlying common stock value has fallen so low that the conversion privilege no longer adds any value to the trading of the bond. In other words, the bond now trades "flat" or just like any other bond of similar quality without a conversion feature.

Of course, you must still like the potential of the company which issued the security. The busted convertible will pay approximately the same interest rate as any nonconvertible bond issued by the same company since it trades at a deep discount. It will react to interest rates like other bonds without conversion privileges.

In general, the common stock price movements will have no bearing on the market price of the busted convertible bond because the common stock price is so far below the conversion price it has no apparent value. The key lies in uncovering companies with the potential to rebound dramatically and having the patience to stick with the busted convertible until better days arrive. Of course, the receipt of competitive interest yields and the potential for significant long-term capital gains can make waiting less of a burden.

A classic busted convertible that came back to life and doubled smart investors' stakes came in the form of Republic Airlines. When the company experienced years of hefty losses, its $1,000 10 1/8 convertible bond traded at a deep discount of 45 percent, meaning you could purchase a $1,000 bond for only $550 each. After Stephen Wolf resurrected Republic Airlines and before he negotiated its sale to Northwest Airlines, the convertible bonds skyrocketed in value to $1,270 per bond. Not only did Republic Airlines convertible bond holders more than double their original investments, they earned a yield in excess of 18 percent while they tracked the progress of the airline's turnaround.

Of course, you could have made more by directly investing in Republic Airlines stock but the bonds gave better investor protection in the event Republic Airlines did have to file for bankruptcy plus you earned over 18 percent interest while management had quit paying dividends on the common stock.

There's always a bevy of companies which have fallen upon tough times. To be sure, some of them will not recover but instead eventually go out of business. However, a little sleuthing and some investigative analysis can help you uncover potential turnaround candidates with busted convertibles ripe for the picking.

Thinly Traded Convertibles

Seeking out inefficiencies in the market is another way to capitalize on convertible bonds. Earlier, we discussed inactive trading in some convertible issues. While this can work to your disadvantage if you need to sell your convertible bonds and you can't find a buyer when you desire or get the price you want, it can also work to your advantage if you have patience and don't need to sell your holdings to raise cash without sufficient advance planning.

Investing in thinly traded convertible securities can put market anomalies in your favor and deliver impressive profits. Placing buy orders several points below current trading levels can let you pick up the convertible bond at a significant discount to its true value when somebody else needs to shed their holdings. It may take awhile to get the order executed but patience is a virtue that pays big dividends.

Likewise, placing sell orders several points above current market prices can also let you pickup additional profits when a buyer places a market buy order for the convertible security.

The time you spend uncovering thinly traded convertibles can be well worth your while in enhanced portfolio gains.

Market Pricing of Convertibles

Market pricing of convertibles takes into account the relationship between the price of the underlying common stock and the conversion value of the convertible security. Figure 3–2, Stock and

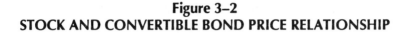

Figure 3–2
STOCK AND CONVERTIBLE BOND PRICE RELATIONSHIP

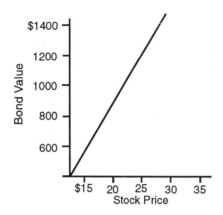

Convertible Bond Price Relationship, illustrates how the value of the bond increases as the price of the underlying common stock rises. Interest rates also come into play as do the earnings prospects of the issuing company.

LOCATING CONVERTIBLE INVESTMENT INFORMATION

Perhaps one of the best places to find information on convertible securities, in addition to your broker, is the *Value Line Convertibles* available from Value Line Publishing, Inc., 711 Third Avenue, New York, New York 10017-4064 or call 1-800-634-3583. An annual subscription for 48 issues costs $475, or you can try a two-month trial subscription for $39.50.

In addition to useful information on call provisions, conversion rates, premium, relative volatility, current yield and yield to maturity, and breakeven time, *Value Line Convertibles* provides a ranking system by which to evaluate convertible issues.

The investment service also provides analysis of and recommendations regarding specific convertibles. For example, the July 5, 1993 issue recommended the Olsten Corporation (AMEX: OLS)

$4.875 of 2003 convertible bond for modest-risk portfolios. It offered participation in the temporary help services firm's upside potential with 45 percent less risk.

COMMON STOCK, CONVERTIBLE, AND STRAIGHT BOND COMPARISONS

Union Carbide Corporation (NYSE: UK) was suffering through its third year of declining profitability in 1991 with a projected loss in excess of 30 cents per share compared to earnings of $5.11 per share as recently as 1988.

Cost cutting and restructuring efforts were underway to improve operations and the company looked to be on the verge of a potential turnaround situation. With a return to a more brisk economy and improved margins, the company had the potential to make giant strides in earnings.

In mid-1991, investors had the choice between the chemical company's common stock which traded around $20 per share and yielded five percent, a straight bond issue of 5.3 percent due in 1997 that traded near par value and yielded 5.3 percent, or a convertible issue of 7.5 percent debentures maturing in 2012 and trading around $770 for a better than 10 percent yield.

How would investors in these three securities have made out? The common stock holders could have made money if they correctly timed their sales and sold out when the company's stock price peaked at $29 5/8 per share in mid-1992. Those that hung on to their shares until mid-August 1993 would have earned an annual yield of five percent but lost money as the stock price sunk to $18 per share as the recession continued.

Investors in the straight bonds would have continued to earn the 5.3 percent yield but with no appreciable capital gain or loss as the bond price more or less treaded water during that time period.

The convertible investors encountered a different scenario. While they started out earning a 10.2 percent yield due to the bond's discount from par, they ran into call provisions which reduced their anticipated investment period and overall yield. With market interest rates declining, the company decided to redeem the high cost convertibles and reduce their interest expense.

The bonds were redeemed on March 16, 1993 at a price of $1038 or the holder had the option of converting to 15.79 shares of common stock. Going the convertible bond route obviously paid off well. Even though the period of earning a high yield of better than 10 percent was cut short by the bond redemption, the capital gain of $268 per bond more than compensated investors.

Another Scenario

Back in early 1991, International Paper Company (NYSE: IP) was having a disasterous year. Earnings were dropping substantially from $6.47 per share in 1990 to an estimated $4.00 per share. Looking ahead, 1992 didn't figure to improve much for the large diversified manufacturer of paper, paperboard, and packaging products.

You knew that as the economy rebounded, International Paper's revenues and earnings prospects would brighten. Unfortunately, your crystal ball did not know when that would happen. You wanted to participate in the cyclical upswing but earning less than three percent on the common stock while the economy turned around did not look very attractive.

Instead, you could have opted to purchase International Paper's 5.75 percent 2002 convertible Eurobonds (available in units of five). These bonds were convertible into 14.599 shares of the company's common stock at a price of $68.50 per share. The convertible issue paid an enticing three percent more yield than the common stock and you still maintained the opportunity to share in the company's upside potential.

In March, 1991, the Eurobonds traded around $1,000 over the counter. In other words, you could earn just under 6 percent and participate in quite a bit of the upside move in the common stock price of International Paper shares but be protected on the downside by the convertible's high yield.

If you took the plunge in March 1991 and purchased the convertible, you would have earned 5.75 percent over the more than two and one-third years through mid-August, 1993 when the bond traded at $105 1/2. So, in addition to the 5 3/4 percent yield you would have also earned a small capital gain of $55 per bond, boosting your overall investment return a bit.

In comparison, International Paper common stock traded around the $64 per share level in March 1991. From there, the stock price rose to a high of $78 1/2 per share in early 1992 before drifting to the $65 3/4 per share level in Mid-August 1993. Under this investment option, you would have earned around a 2.7 percent yield plus a same capital gain on the $1 3/4 rise in the firm's common stock price.

Clearly, the convertible option paid off better in the long run. However, there was also another investment alternative to consider. This consisted of purchasing the deeply discounted straight 5 1/8 percent International Paper bonds which traded around $630 each for a $1,000 face value bond.

Due to the deep discount, these bonds yielded over 8.2 percent. By mid-August, 1993, in the wake of declining market interest rates, the bond's market price had recovered to $810. In this instance, purchasing the straight bonds paid off more handsomely than buying either the common stock or the convertible issue.

This stresses the importance on not getting too enamored by any particular investment method or investment security. As a savvy investor, you must investigate the different alternatives and analyze the potential gains and risks associated with each.

OTHER CONVERTIBLE WRINKLES

A number of corporations have introduced zero coupon convertible bonds in recent years. These will be discussed in Chapter 10, Zeroing in on Zeros.

More recently, companies have issued what have been termed 'step-up' convertibles ('SIRENS' Step-up Income Redeemable Equity Notes) in efforts to raise money with lower interest rates. The step-up convertible works like this. Unlike traditional convertibles which pay a fixed rate of interest until maturity, redemption, or conversion, the step-ups possess a two-tiered interest rate structure.

The issuing firm pays a below-market interest rate during the early years of the issue and a higher rate for the remaining life of the security. The attraction from the company's perspective is obvious—lower upfront borrowing costs, sometimes as low as below four percent as in the case of Horace Mann Educators Corporation.

From the investor's perspective, the blended rate results in an overall yield higher than the going market rate, plus they still have the option to convert to stock should the common stock price rise dramatically. If the conversion takes place before the step-up in interest rate occurs, the company benefits from not having to pay the higher rate.

It's too early to tell how well these new convertible securities will hold up in the secondary market but they should be watched with interest.

Global Convertible Securities

"There's an overwhelming need for capital worldwide with increasing globilization and emerging markets. U.S. investors don't think globally enough. International convertible securities represent a natural stepping stone for U.S. investors to increase their international exposure. They offer high current yields compared to international common stocks and are issued by blue chip companies with excellent credit quality and the largest capitalization of overseas companies," says Michael D. Rodier, a vice president with Wellington Management Company in Boston, Massachusetts.

Rodier sees unique convertible investment opportunities in the international arena because the international market is not yet as sophisticated in valuing convertible securities. Likewise, many convertible issues from one country are virtually ignored by investors in other overseas countries. Therefore, undervalued situations can be found.

You don't have to worry about dealing in foreign currencies either. Many international convertibles are denominated in U.S. dollars with both the coupon interest and principal paid in U.S. currency. As with any foreign investment, you still undertake foreign currency risk, but this is tempered somewhat by the U.S. dollar denomination.

The Eurobond market offers relatively efficient settlement and high liquidity. Most large global convertible securities are Eurobonds and thus free from withholding tax for interest and dividends.

Convertible Mutual Funds

A number of mutual funds specialize exclusively in convertible securities while many others hold convertible issues in their portfolios to enhance yield and potential capital gains.

According to Morningstar Rating Service in Chicago, Illinois, for the 12-month period through July 31, 1993 convertible funds (25 funds) delivered a return of 17.10 percent versus only 10.23 percent for general corporate bond funds (168 funds) and 12.52 percent for growth stock funds (444 funds).

Tops among the convertible funds in 1992 were Fidelity Convertible Securities with a 22 percent return, Putnam Convertible Income Growth Trust with a 21 percent advance and Vanguard Convertible with a 19 percent return.

Fidelity's long-term track record is impressive as well. For the five-year time frame, the Fidelity Convertible Securities Fund earned an average annual return of 18.6 percent compared with 15.6 percent for the S&P 500.

The funds in Table 3–1 target the convertible securities market as their main investment thrust.

Besides the mutual fund route to convertible investing, there are a number of closed-end convertible securities funds which

Table 3–1
CONVERTIBLE SECURITIES FUNDS

Fund	Telephone Number
AIM Convertible Securities	800-347-1919
American Capital Harbor A & B	800-421-5666
CFS: Calamos Convertible	800-323-9943
Convertible Sec & Inc.	800-245-4770
Dean Witter Convertible Securities	800-869-3863
Dreyfus Convertible Securities	800-782-6620
Fidelity Convertible Securities Fund	800-544-8888
Franklin Inv: Convertible Securities	800-342-5236
Gabelli Convertible Securities	800-422-3554
Harris Insight: Convertible	800-441-7379
Institutional Inv Convertible Sec	212-551-1920
Lexington Convertible Securities	800-526-0056
Mainstay Convertible	800-522-4202
Merrill Global Convertible A & B	800-637-3863
Pacific Horizon: Capital Income	800-332-3863
Phoenix Convertible	800-243-4361
Putnam Convertible Inc Growth Trust	800-225-1581
Retire Plan Amer: Convertible	800-279-0279
Rochester Convertible	716-383-1300
SBSF Convertible Securities	800-422-7273
Smith Barney Shearson Convertible	800-544-7835
Value Line Convertible	800-662-7447
Vanguard Convertible	800-662-7447

Table 3–2
CLOSED-END CONVERTIBLE SECURITIES FUNDS

Fund	Exchange	Symbol
American Capital Convertible	NYSE	ACS
Bancroft Convertible	AMEX	BCV
Castle Convertible	AMEX	CVF
Ellsworth Convertible	AMEX	ECF
Lincoln National Convertible	NYSE	LNV
Putnam Hi In Convertible	NYSE	PCF
TCW Convertible	NYSE	CVT

trade on the New York and American exchanges (Table 3–2). See Chapter Two, ADRs and Other Global Investing Options for a discussion of closed-end funds.

Convertible securities make excellent investment choices when the market is in turmoil and the direction of individual company stock prices remains uncertain. Sit back and enjoy a higher yield than available on the common stock but still maintain a degree of upside potential with reduced risk on the downside.

4

managing margin

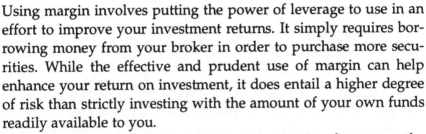

Using margin involves putting the power of leverage to use in an effort to improve your investment returns. It simply requires borrowing money from your broker in order to purchase more securities. While the effective and prudent use of margin can help enhance your return on investment, it does entail a higher degree of risk than strictly investing with the amount of your own funds readily available to you.

Before you embark on using margin, you need to assess the risks involved and your own risk posture. Remember, using margin leverage creates greater opportunities for both larger profits and losses, therefore, putting you in a riskier position than non-leveraged securities purchases. With that in mind, let's take a look at how a margin account works and how it can improve your investment returns.

Typically, an investor purchases securities with available cash in his or her brokerage account, paying for the purchase within the five day period required under securities regulations.

Using the other guy's money (your broker's) can represent an effective way to significantly increase your investment returns. With margin, you can purchase more shares of a particular security with the same amount of cash outlay. If you analyzed the situation right and the stock rises as anticipated, your return on investment and capital gains can multiply at a substantial clip.

Under Federal Reserve Regulation T, which regulates the minimum margin requirements, the investor must deposit a specified amount of cash and/or equity represented by security holdings as collateral for margined purchases. Since 1974, minimum margin requirements have stood at 50 percent, meaning your broker can lend you up to 50 percent of the stock's value.

The minimum equity value that must be maintained in a margin account is termed margin maintenance. Regulation T requires a deposit of a minimum $2,000 before any margin credit can be extended by the brokerage firm to the investor. In addition, individual brokerage houses may impose stricter initial and minimum margin requirements as a matter of company policy. These restrictions are known as house maintenance requirements.

Of course, there is no free lunch. Just as when you borrow from a bank or use your credit cards for purchases, the financial institution charges you interest. Your margin account with your broker works like a line of credit and the brokerage firm will also charge your account margin interest on outstanding balances.

Brokerage firms calculate the rate they charge you based on a number of factors including the "broker call rate," what banks charge brokerage firms for lending them the money that they in turn lend to you. On top of that, brokerages add anywhere from one-quarter to two percentage points, depending on how much you borrow.

To make a good investment decision, compare the cost of borrowing money from your broker with the interest charged on a commercial loan or your credit cards. In mid-July 1993, Merrill Lynch charged a margin interest rate of 8.25 percent for margin loans up to $9,000, 8.00 percent on margin loans from $10,000 to $24,999, and 7.375 percent on margin loans from $25,000 to $49,999. That compares to credit card rates ranging anywhere from 12 to over 20 percent and home mortgage rates and personal credit line rates on second mortgages around nine percent.

It also pays to shop around. Discount broker, Waterhouse Securities, Inc., at the same time charged six percent for margin loans up to $49,999 and 5.5 percent for margin loans $50,000 and over.

When you consider your cost of money, it's important to remember the tax implications. Tax legislation that took effect January 1, 1987, had some unintentioned effects. Under that legislation, margin loans are still tax deductible, up to the amount of net investment income; therefore, they possess a tax advantage over other forms of credit. You can no longer use the interest charges on personal bank loans, credit cards, or automobile loans as a deduction to reduce your income tax liability.

Obviously, one possible way to offset the tax restrictions on interest deductions is to use your broker's money to purchase securities. The interest charged will be tax deductible, assuming your investment gain exceeds the margin interest charged on your margin purchases. However, a caveat is in order. Don't let tax considerations cloud your investment decisions and risk posture. Make investment decisions, such as whether or not to use margin, based on an investment analysis of risk and opportunities. Then, if the tax situation works out, all the better.

There are also some guidelines to follow to make sure you don't run afoul of the IRS. The margin loan proceeds must be used for investment purposes. Therefore, don't go out and borrow money against securities already in your account and use the money for a shopping spree thinking you can use the tax deduction. If you do, you may find yourself facing an IRS audit and interest and penalties on any disclaimed interest deduction. Let discretion be the better part of valor. Check with your accountant or tax consultant before you make any major investment interest tax deduction moves.

In addition, the IRS places some limits on the amount of margin interest you can deduct in any one year. Interest not allowed by the limitation may be carried forward and deducted from next year's net investment income. You can deduct investment interest up to the level of net investment income which is defined as gross investment income less investment expenses (excluding investment interest) after figuring the two percent floor for miscellaneous itemized deductions. The two percent floor will bar the deduction of some miscellaneous investment expenses.

The following example illustrates how your deductible margin investment interest would be calculated.

Assume you borrow $20,000 to purchase securities and pay margin interest of $1,600 over the span of the tax year. Fortunately, you made money on the security purchases and sales to the tune of $1,500 during the year. Accordingly, you can deduct $1,500 as allowable investment interest against this year's net investment income. The balance will be carried forward to next year.

You may have paper gains in excess of the $1,500 profit but until you sell the security or securities, you can only use the margin investment interest to offset against actualized gains.

See Figure 4-1, Form 4952 Investment Interest Expense Deduction, for an example of how to show the amount of margin investment interest allowable on your federal tax return.

As you can see, you can only deduct $1,500 of your $1,600 in investment interest paid out during the current tax year (up to

Figure 4-1
INVESTMENT INTEREST EXPENSE DEDUCTION

Form **4952**	**Investment Interest Expense Deduction**	OMB No. 1545-0191
Department of the Treasury Internal Revenue Service	▶ Attach to your tax return.	1992 Attachment Sequence No. **72**
Name(s) shown on return		Identifying number

1	Investment interest expense paid or accrued in 1992. See instructions	**1**	1,600 00
2	Disallowed investment interest expense from 1991 Form 4952, line 5	**2**	
3	Total investment interest expense. Add lines 1 and 2	**3**	1,600 00
4	**Net investment income.** See instructions	**4**	1,500 00
5	**Disallowed investment interest expense to be carried forward to 1993.** Subtract line 4 from line 3. If zero or less, enter -0-	**5**	100 00
6	**Investment interest expense deduction.** Enter the smaller of line 3 or line 4. See instructions	**6**	1,500 00

the amount of your net investment income). The balance of $100 in investment interest gets carried over into the next tax year.

HOW MARGIN WORKS

Understanding how margin works provides insight into the advantages and risks associated with using margin. This in turn gives you a perspective to see how, and if, margin investing fits your investment goals and risk tolerance.

As mentioned earlier, investors borrow from their brokers on margin by placing cash and/or securities in their margin account as collateral for the loan. It is important to note that not all securities are marginable. Typically, brokers will not accept stock trading below $10 per share, but some brokers will accept stock trading above $5 per share on margin. However, most New York Stock Exchange, American Stock Exchange and many OTC stocks can be margined.

All brokerage margin customers are required to sign a margin agreement spelling out the terms of the loan, margin maintenance requirements, and other details of the loan agreement. Remember, your broker is bound by law to completely comply with the terms of the margin agreement. There is absolutely no room for leeway or negotiation.

The margin agreement spells out in detail what actions will be taken in the event your account falls below minimum margin requirements and you do not correct the situation within the time limit specified. Don't just sign on the dotted line without thoroughly reading and comprehending the margin agreement and the ramifications of dropping below minimum maintenance levels. You can save yourself a lot of headaches, sleepless nights, and plenty of money by knowing the margin rules and keeping your margin account within the required limits.

Brokerage firms continuously monitor minimum margin maintenance levels. Should your account fall below the minimum, your broker will immediately send out a "margin call" letter similar to the following:

Due to recent market action and in accordance with federal margin regulations, it will be necessary for you to deposit with our firm as soon as possible, but in any event before (date), the sum of (amount), or acceptable securities having a loan value of at least that amount.

The margin call may take the form of a letter, telephone call (followed up with written correspondence), or a telegram but the message is the same . . . send money or securities of equal value.

In plain English, this call letter is a serious shot across the bow telling you to bring your margin account into compliance with federal regulations immediately. The next shot will not be across the bow but right through the heart of your margined portfolio.

If you fail to meet the demands of the margin call in time, your broker will sell out enough of your stock positions to raise the required cash to bring your account back into compliance. Needless to say, you could suffer substantial losses if your positions are liquidated at an inopportune time, even though the downturn in your portfolio value may be short-lived in today's volatile stock markets.

Guard against this grim scenario by properly maintaining your collateral level and promptly responding to any margin calls. If you decide to invest using margin, you should have adequate cash reserves, assets readily converted to cash, and/or borrowing capacity in order to meet any margin calls should the market turn down and your margin portfolio drops in value below minimum margin requirements.

Obviously, one risk of trading on margin lies in the possibility of being forced to sell out positions at the wrong time due to margin requirements. Another risk stems from overextending yourself and purchasing more securities than are prudent for your financial position. Remember, leverage works both ways, your investment losses under margin mount up faster if the stock prices of the securities you purchase on margin decline.

Now, if you have not been scared away by the very real risks and dangers of trading on margin, let's take a look at how the prudent use of margin can improve your investment performance.

First of all, investment margin interest is fully deductible (up to the level of your net investment income). This allows you to free up cash for other purposes plus maintain an allowable interest expense tax deduction (in the wake of Congress eliminating many other interest tax deductions).

The second and major lure of using margin comes from the power of using leverage (other people's money) to earn investment gains. By using margin, you can double the amount of securities you purchase for the same amount of your cash investment. Or looking at it another way, you can purchase the same dollar amount of securities for half the investment, assuming a 50 percent margin rate.

Having a margin account allows you to take advantage of unique and temporary market opportunities even though you may not have cash available in your account. Using securities in your margin account, you can purchase additional securities without putting up additional cash.

Initial margin requirements may vary depending on the type of investment being purchased. For example, while federal regulations and brokerage houses require at least a 50 percent initial margin requirement for equities, initial margin requirements for corporate non-convertible bonds stand at 30 percent and for United States Treasury bills or notes the rate is 8 percent and 10 percent for U.S. Treasury bonds. Different brokerage firms may have higher house requirements.

To illustrate the significant amount of leverage available and how it can be used to enhance your portfolio return consider the following examples.

Case Study #1

Assume you have $50,000 to invest. You have been tracking the fortunes of ABC company and the industry in which it operates and believe its earnings are positioned for a big jump over prior year levels and expect the firm's stock market price to follow suit and spurt ahead several points above its current trading level in the near future. In addition, you anticipate ABC's stock price will then trend steadily upward from there over the next three-to-five year time horizon.

Ignoring commissions and investment interest, at a current market price of $20 per share, you can purchase 2,500 shares of ABC Company stock. Now, if the stock jumps as you anticipate to $28 per share, your investment gain will total $7,500 ($3 × 2,500) for a 15 percent immediate return ($7,500/$50,000). Your annual return will depend on how long it took to obtain the $3 per share gain and how much more the stock advances in the remainder of the year.

Now, if you had used margin to purchase twice as many shares for the same $50,000 cash investment, your portfolio return would calculate to be much higher. Under this scenario, you could purchase 5,000 shares of ABC stock. Your profit would now amount to $15,000 ($3 × 5,000), or a doubling of your profit under the straight cash investing approach. Likewise, using leverage boosted your return on investment to 30 percent ($15,000/$50,000).

Case Study #2

This time, assume you purchase the same number of shares (2,500) as you would under the straight cash approach. While the purchase cost of the 2,500 share stake remains $50,000 ($20 × 2,500), using margin, you only have to ante up $25,000 or 50 percent of the stock's value. You can use the balance of your $25,000 cash for other purposes.

Again, as under the previous case study, ABC's stock prices rises to $28 per share. The $3 rise per share translates into a $7,500 ($3 × 2,500) investment gain, the same profit as in the straight cash purchase example. However, instead of earning a return of investment of 15 percent, you have boosted your investment return results to 30 percent ($7,500/$25,000). That's double the investment return of purchasing the shares for cash.

There is a substantial difference between your investment performance derived from using leverage and the leverage of using other people's money to purchase stock on margin. There are some other differences as well.

You incur interest expenses when using margin. This expense cuts into your investment return. One way to help blunt the impact of investment interest on portfolio performance is to invest in stocks with dividends that at least partially offset the margin interest charges.

The other major difference between the straight cash investing approach and margined security purchases stems from the level of risk you assume.

A volatile or declining stock market can jeopardize your margin holdings. If your stock falls in value enough, your margin collateral may not be enough to keep you within minimum margin requirements, triggering a margin call letter, or even worse, a liquidation of some or all of your security holdings in the margin account.

Taking a look at another example will clearly point out the risks of employing margin in an attempt to bolster your overall investment performance.

Case Study #3

Assume you use your $50,000 in cash to purchase $100,000 worth of ABC Company stock at $20 per share, under the 50 percent margin requirement. Your $100,000 worth of purchasing power allows you to acquire 5,000 shares ($100,000/$20). An earthquake hits California and destroys ABC's major plant, accounting for more than 70 percent of company production capacity. Worse yet, it looks like it will take months before the company can expand capacity at other facilities or repair the damage to the California plant to resume production levels. As a result, the company's bright prospects have turned into a loss situation and a potential of market share on a permanent basis.

As expected, investors react negatively to the news and the company's bleak prospects. The company's stock price takes an immediate nose dive, slashing $3 per share off the market price.

This results in a loss of $15,000 ($3 × 5,000). The percentage decline in the value of your holdings calculates to 15 percent ($15,000/$100,000); however, your loss on investment leaps to 30 percent ($15,000/$50,000). That's how leverage works on the downside.

In comparison, if you had used your $50,000 nest egg to purchase shares on a cash basis, you would have only bought 2,500 shares. In this more conservative cash purchase scenario, your loss would be only $7,500 ($3 × 2,500), half of the loss incurred by using margin. In the same vein, your loss on your investment would also be substantially less, 15 percent ($7,500/$50,000) versus the 30 percent loss suffered using margin.

The loss would be bad enough but if the value of your overall margin collateral fell below the minimum requirement, the broker would issue a margin call requiring you to ante up adequate additional funds or securities to raise your collateral level up to acceptable limits. In the above example, let's assume that above and beyond the $50,000 in cash deposited with the broker to purchase the $100,000 in ABC Company shares that you also had another $10,000 in value in securities in your margin account.

Therefore, your total margin account valuation after you purchased the ABC shares stood at $110,000 ($100,000 + $10,000). After the $3 drop in the per share price of ABC stock, your margin account valuation fell to $95,000 ($17 × 5,000 + $10,000). The marginable value of your collateral has dropped to $47,500 ($95,000 × .50). Unfortunately, your margin loan totals $50,000.

Your options include depositing $2,500 in cash and/or acceptable securities valued at least that much to get back within the 50 percent margin minimum.

Failing to receive the appropriate amount of cash or securities, the broker is bound to liquidate enough of your margin holdings to raise the cash and bring your account back into compliance. It's doubtful you will be asked which stocks you may wish to keep. The results could be disastrous.

As you can see, using margin is not for the timid investor. It can be utilized effectively to boost investment returns but major risks exist. Only you can decide whether or not margin investing fits your investment strategy and risk parameters.

There are several things you can do to reduce the risk of receiving a margin call. Spreading your security purchases into a well-balanced, diversified stock portfolio provides a measure of safety since a drop in the price of one or two stocks is unlikely to prompt a margin call. Upward moves in the prices of the other holdings will support the overall valuation.

Maintaining a diversified margin portfolio reduces the risk that a decline in any one industry or market sector will raise havoc with margin levels. Another recommended margin strategy consists of purchasing stocks on margin that tend to move in different cycles than the securities being used as collateral. This tactic helps prevent both the margined stocks and collateral holdings from taking a nosedive at the same time.

Watching economic and stock cycles also pays off. While holding cyclical stocks during a rising cycle may make good sense, get out before the industry starts peaking and the market action rotates to yet another stock group.

Beyond diversification, it's important to maintain a conservative posture in your margin investing. Don't operate fully margined. Borrowing less than the 50 percent allowable margin gives you a cushion in the event stock prices drop or rise and then fall in a volatile market environment.

For example, if you only borrow 30 percent on the value of a stock trading at $50 per share instead of the maximum 50 percent, the market price would have to drop below $30 a share or 40 percent from its purchase price before margin value levels would trigger a margin call.

Don't buy stocks on margin and forget about them. You need to track your investments and margin status on a regular basis to ensure you don't get caught short by a margin call. If you see the value of your account is getting dangerously close to the minimum margin required, you still have time to take defensive action. Reposition your portfolio or raise the cash necessary to avert a margin call or your securities from being sold out from under you.

The use of stop-loss orders can be an effective tool to help you avoid dramatic losses and margin calls. The stop-loss is an order placed with your broker to protect existing gains or limit losses. It works like this. You instruct your broker to set a sell price for the specific security at a price below the current market price. When the stock's market price drops to the stop-loss price you set, the order becomes a market order, allowing you to close out your position and prevent any further losses and possibly avoid a margin call.

It's wise to maintain a safety cushion of readily available funds or borrowing capacity to meet the demands of your broker to beef up your margin account value.

Stock picking tactics for margin candidates requires a slightly different tact than you use for making purchases in your cash account. While you can ride out the ups and downs of volatile securities in your cash account, a sudden drop, although only temporary, in the stock price could set off a margin call and even a forced sale of securities if you are unprepared to bring in an infusion of cash or securities to beef up the margin account's valuation.

Of course, in your efforts to remove volatility, you still need to discover margin stock candidates that promise to move upward in price. When a stock's price remains steady or declines, the margin investor continues to incur interest charges, a drag on investment income and portfolio returns. The stock must have the potential to rise enough to cover the commission and interest charges.

These are the basics for margin investing. More sophisticated investing strategies involving margin include short selling (which will be covered in Chapter Eight, Selling Short) and options (which will be covered in (Chapter Six, Options).

From a market perspective, the level of market debt often signals investor confidence in the direction of the market. As investors believe more and more in a stronger market, they vote their confidence by purchasing additional securities on margin. Traditionally, there has been a fast build-up of margin debt in bull markets and a sharp decline in margin debt during bear markets.

Falling prices create margin calls, which in turn force investors to sell out margined positions, thus fueling the downward price spiral. On the upside, rising use of margin creates demand for stocks, causing their price to rise even higher.

Keeping a pulse on changes in margin levels can help signal market direction changes in the making. Using a six-month moving average eliminates any temporary blips in margin numbers. A rising moving average confirms an increasing stock market while a declining average or trendline confirms a falling market.

AN HISTORICAL VIEW

The imprudent use of margin in the late 1920s is often cited as one of the main reasons for the precipitous crash of the stock market starting in 1929. Indeed, astute and novice investors alike purchased stock with as little as 10 percent down, expecting stock prices to continue their heady rise experienced earlier in the decade.

In 1929, more margin trading took place than in any other year in the history of the country. Forty percent of all customers purchased stocks on margin.

After the crash, jurisdiction over margin requirements came under the authority of the Federal Reserve Board with passage of the Securities Exchange Act of 1934. The legislation gave the

Board the power to control margins by regulating the maximum credit that can be extended on registered securities.

Regulation T controls the extension and maintenance of credit to customers by brokers, dealers, and members of national securities exchanges. Regulation U governs the loans by banks for the purpose of purchasing stocks registered on the national securities exchanges.

The Federal Reserve Board changed the margin percentage 23 times from the period 1934 to date with the last change occurring on January 3, 1974, when it reduced the margin percent requirement to 50 percent from 65 percent. Since 1934, the minimum margin percent was as low as 25 percent in 1934 (depending on present price to lowest price ratio on each security) to as high as 100 percent during the January 21, 1946 through January 31, 1947 period.

If the Board feels market speculation is getting too rampant, it moves to curtail the amount of capital available for investment. It accomplishes this by raising the minimum margin percent requirement. On the other hand, it will reduce the margin percent to expand available capital.

EMPLOYING THE MARGIN STRATEGY

Use the following steps in instituting your own margin strategy:

- Fully understand how margin works, both on the upside and the downside.

- Develop a margin investing strategy consistent with your investment goals and risk tolerance.

- Investigate your margin costs and shop around. Each brokerage house calculates margin interest differently.

- Request a copy of the margin agreement from your broker.

- Study the agreement and understand how it works before you sign it.

- Tell the broker how much you want to borrow.

- Specify which stocks you want to purchase on margin.

- Track your margin purchases and margin account valuation.

The choice to use margin or not is up to you. It possesses tremendous potential to increase investment returns but not without added risk. Deciding to use margin should be done just like you make any investment decision, only after carefully weighing all the facts.

5

minding metals

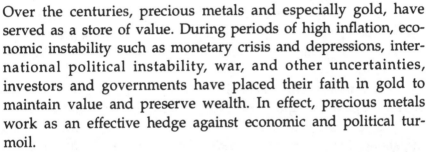

Over the centuries, precious metals and especially gold, have served as a store of value. During periods of high inflation, economic instability such as monetary crisis and depressions, international political instability, war, and other uncertainties, investors and governments have placed their faith in gold to maintain value and preserve wealth. In effect, precious metals work as an effective hedge against economic and political turmoil.

In addition to preserving purchasing power, maintaining value, and providing a safe haven in troubled times, precious metals also serve other economic purposes. Heavy demand for gold and other precious metals translates into upward price pressure as industrial and ornamental use increases.

For example, both gold and silver are used extensively as jewelry or other ornamental adornments. Likewise, various industries use gold, silver, platinum, palladium, and other precious metals for industrial production of everything from electronics to sophisticated military equipment. Many precious metals are becoming increasingly vital to new technological applications.

CHAPTER FIVE

GOLD—ALL THAT GLITTERS

During the high inflation and turbulent times of the late 1970s and early 1980s, gold fever grew to historic proportions.

As indicated above, the reason for the volatility of gold prices stems from uncertainty. Gold serves as a storehouse of value when the purchasing power of money declines. Faced with interest rates above 20 percent, inflation rates in the double digits, economic concerns, surging oil prices, and international political unrest, investors and speculators pushed gold prices to record highs around $850 per ounce in 1980, more than doubling its 1979 average price level around $306 per ounce.

Since the early 1980s, gold prices have drifted lower. Gold prices bottomed out in 1985 at a price of $284 per ounce, before settling into a decade-long price range between $400 and $335 per ounce with an occasional run at the $500 per ounce level as we neared the 1990s. In fact, many gold bugs deserted gold as inflation dropped to the three percent level and an international recession fell into place.

After more than a decade of drifting gold prices, investors are once again sitting up and taking notice of this versatile metal. From a low of $326 per ounce in March, gold bullion prices threatened to push through the $400 per ounce threshold in early July, 1993.

Likewise, the prices of gold stocks started appearing in the most active lists on U.S. exchanges and gold mutual funds for the first quarter of 1993 turned in a glittering performance, earning a return of nearly 22 percent versus just a tad over three percent for the average stock mutual fund.

Why all the sudden interest in gold investments and how best can the individual investor participate in future gold moves?

Concerns over inflation rearing its ugly head once again, the aging bull market in stocks and bonds, loss of confidence in the central banks and major currencies, political and economic instability, rising gold demand, and outbreaks of wars in former Yugoslavia, Somalia, and possible upheaval in South Africa combined to push the price of gold to highs around $397 per ounce by early

July 1993, the highest price level since the Gulf War in January 1991.

A number of factors exerted upward pressure on gold prices in the first half of 1993, but before we look at the future prospects for gold prices, we'll first take a look at historical gold prices and various ways you can participate in gold investments.

Table 5-1 reflects the range of gold prices over the past dozen years.

Table 5-1
GOLD PRICES PER TROY OUNCE*

Year	High	Low
1980	$850	$482
1981	599	391
1982	481	297
1983	509	374
1984	406	308
1985	341	284
1986	438	327
1987	502	389
1988	487	392
1989	419	356
1990	425	346
1991	403	341
1992	362	335
1993	397	326
		through early July 1993

* Gold Prices in U.S. Dollars London P.M. Fix, Yearly

Figure 5-1, Gold Chart, shows gold price action from the low in March 1993, to the high in early July 1993. Gold futures pricing and contracts from *Investor's Business Daily's* July 12, 1993, issue reflect investor interest and sentiment about future gold pricing. See Figure 5-2, Gold Futures.

Figure 5–1
GOLD CHART

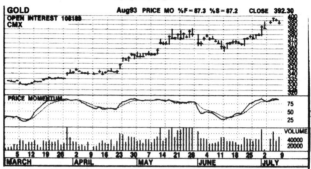

Source: *Investor's Business Daily*, July 1993.

Reprinted with permission of *Investor's Business Daily*.

With the exception of the high inflationary period of the early 1980s, over the years, the price of gold bullion has kept pace with inflation. See Figure 5–3, Gold Bullion Compared with Inflation, to see how gold stacked up against inflation for the period 1978 through mid-1992.

Figure 5–2
GOLD FUTURES

PRECIOUS METALS

GOLD (CMX) – 100 troy oz. – dollars per troy oz.
Est. Vol. 50,000 Vol. 35,458 open int 201,973 + 1,143

428.00 366.50 Jul	10				391.60	– 3.30
426.50 328.50 Aug	108,189	392.00	394.70	390.80	392.30	– 3.30
397.80 388.00 Sep	· 3	393.50	394.50	393.50	393.30	– 3.30
400.50 330.80 Oct	6,295	393.50	397.40	393.00	394.40	– 3.30
402.40 331.70 Dec	40,604	396.00	398.80	395.00	396.40	– 3.30
404.00 333.80 Feb	12,619	398.50	400.30	397.30	398.10	– 3.30
406.00 335.20 Apr	6,269	400.00	402.30	398.40	399.80	– 3.30
406.40 339.40 Jun	5,182	402.50	402.50	400.30	401.60	– 3.20
408.80 341.50 Aug	2,797				403.40	– 3.20
408.50 344.00 Oct					405.30	– 3.20
413.00 343.00 Dec	9,598	407.00	409.60	406.50	407.40	– 3.20
400.00 368.00 Feb					409.70	– 3.20
412.50 390.20 Apr	388				412.10	– 3.20
420.00 411.50 Jun		414.00	414.00	414.00	414.60	– 3.20

Source: *Investor's Business Daily*, July 1993.

Reprinted with permission of *Investor's Business Daily*.

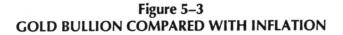

Figure 5–3
GOLD BULLION COMPARED WITH INFLATION

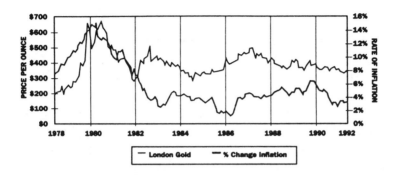

Despite its recent lackluster performance, with the recent exception of the mid-1993 price spurt, gold has been attractive to investors for the following reasons.

■ Its scarcity translates higher demand into higher gold prices.

■ Vast wealth can be concentrated in small quantities of the metal.

■ Gold can be easily transported or exchanged for value.

■ Gold is readily accepted as an international medium of exchange.

■ Gold reacts to unsettling international incidents which tend to destabilize other forms of value or investments such as paper currency and stocks and bonds.

■ Gold appeals aesthetically to people who desire it for its beauty as jewelry or other adornments.

■ Rising industrial applications adds unlimited demand potential as uses for gold expands in new and exotic industries.

GOLD INVESTMENT ALTERNATIVES

A variety of ways exist in which to invest in gold, each with its
own set of risks and opportunities for capital gains. You can construct your gold portfolio and gold investing strategy from gold
bullion in the form of bars or ingots to gold bullion coins to
shares of gold mining stocks or mutual funds that specialize in
gold investments to gold jewelry to gold futures.

Gold investing can run the gamut from taking a conservative
stance to a high risk speculative posture with corresponding opportunities for extraordinary gains. Each method of gold investment possesses its own unique advantages or disadvantages.
Investors must decide for themselves which type of gold investment, if any, makes the best sense for their overall investment
strategy.

Typically, many investment advisors recommend that an investor maintain at least a three to five percent position in gold at
all times in order to help keep pace with inflation and provide a
hedge against economic uncertainty.

Bullion

The most practical form of gold holdings for governments, gold
bullion bars or ingots, is probably the least convenient for the individual investor. Bullion bars can be purchased in sizes as small
as one gram. One of the problems with investing in bullion bars
is that they must be re-assayed to ascertain weight and purity
before they can be resold. The re-assay process and costs can be
side-stepped if you store the bars in a bonded warehouse or de-
pository bank, either in the United States or overseas.

Storage costs and insurance also add to the cost of investing in gold bullion and reduce your overall return. If you opt to take delivery of the gold bullion, you will also incur some nominal delivery fees. As a whole, these delivery, storage, and insurance costs can amount to one percent of the value of the gold.

Liquidity can also come into play when investing in bullion bars. Since bullion bars are typically sold in large quantities, a desire to sell a few bullion bars could face small public demand.

In addition, bullion in small units typically carries a stiff premium, decreasing your return potential.

Gold Certificates

For those investors who desire to hold ownership interests in gold bullion but don't want to deal with the hassles of delivery, assaying, lugging around gold ingots, etc., innovative investment firms have developed the gold certificate.

Simply stated, gold certificates represent ownership of gold stored at a custodial depositary. Advantages include ease of transfer, avoidance of the physical problems of owning gold and safekeeping concerns, and elimination of the need for re-assaying the gold before sale. Certificates represent your gold ownership but since they are non-negotiable they provide a level of security. They cannot be sold, assigned, or transferred without your specific written request.

You still incur a custodial fee which covers costs for storage, insuring of the gold, record-keeping, and authentification.

Generally, gold certificates are purchased at the current spot price of gold. However, the custodial fees mentioned above can run another one percent of the value of the gold.

Reflecting the popularity on gold certificates, 75 percent of the gold investors at one major brokerage firm chose the certificate route.

Gold and Silver Bullion

Gold bullion coins represent a gold investment with a unique twist. On top of their reaction to gold prices in general, gold bullion coins derive price changes from shifts in investor sentiment over the relative value of particular collector coins in relation to other collector coins, both gold and otherwise.

Gold bullion coins gain favor among investors for several reasons. They are small and much easier to transport and store than their gold bullion bar and ingot counterparts. Gold coins can be purchased in a variety of convenient sizes with the most common ranging from one-tenth of an ounce to one ounce coins. Bullion coins also deliver a great deal of liquidity since they are traded almost anywhere in the world. Remember that the smaller coins typically carry higher premiums because their per unit production costs are correspondingly higher than that of the larger coins.

Among the most popular legal tender coins are the silver American Eagle, U.S. $50 Gold Eagles, U.S. $25 Gold Eagles, Canadian Silver Maple Leafs, Platinum Maple Leafs, Chinese Panda, English Platinum Noble, and South African Krugerrands. Although the United States banned the import of South African Krugerrands back in the mid-1980s for political purposes, trading of Krugerrands already in the U.S. market at the time of imposition of the ban can be conducted by investors.

Typically, premiums on the more popular gold coins run from three to five percent.

Moving into the collector arena, you need to seek out the advice of a reputable professional coin dealer. There are a lot of different grades and prices for collector coins and it's easy for the novice coin investor to get burned.

Collector coins provide an opportunity for faster appreciation and profits, but that comes with a higher degree of volatility and risk. Mint quantities become important in the valuation of collector coins. All other things being equal, a coin with a lower mint quantity will command a higher price due to the classic demand and supply equation.

As a general rule, prices of collector (numismatic) coins tend to advance faster than bullion coins in a rising market and decline more slowly during a down market. Traditionally, collector coins have performed exceptionally well in inflationary times and have held their value in deflationary times due to their collector value.

However, collector coins typically run into a less liquid market than bullion coins. Since more of their value is based upon changing investor sentiment, it is harder to find a willing buyer and establish a firm value.

Investment performance in coins runs in cycles just like other investments. For the 15 year period 1971–1985, United States investment quality coins earned 18 percent on an average annual basis, outperforming other investment alternatives.

Table 5–2 shows the relative performance of different classes of investments for the 1971–1985 time frame.

Table 5–2
INVESTMENT RATES OF RETURN
1971–1985 AVERAGE

Investment Class	Annual Return
1. U.S. Coins	18%
2. Gold	15
3. Stamps	14
4. Oil	13
5. Diamonds	10
6. Stocks	10
7. Bonds	9
8. Treasury Bills	8
9. Silver	8
10. Real Estate	8

A variety of coins continue to do well. The Blanchard and Company's Index of Mint State Gold Coins returned a 29.5 percent return in 1992. See Figure 5–4, Blanchard Mint State Gold Index. Blanchard is the nation's largest retailer of PCGS (Profes-

Figure 5–4
BLANCHARD MINT STATE GOLD INDEX

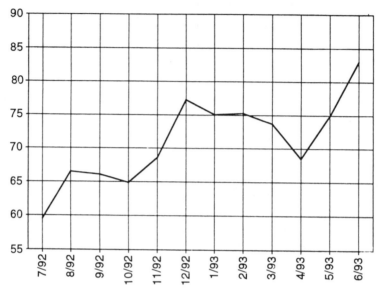

Source: Blanchard and Company.

sional Coin Grading Service) and NGC (Numismatic Guarantee Corporation) certified rare U.S. coins and the publisher of *The Consumer's Guide to Coin Investing and Collecting*, in conjunction with the U.S. Postal Service. To request a copy, call 800-880-4653, or write to Blanchard and Company, P. O. Box 61740, New Orleans, Louisiana 70161-1740.

You need to be aware of a few numismatic basics to effectively participate in the world of collector coin investing. The coin's mint mark denotes which mint struck the coin. This is important because the value of the same denomination and year coin can vary significantly based on its mint mark. Typically, this variation depends on mint quantity, but not always.

You can locate the majority of mint marks on the reverse (tail) side of the coin. Any good coin book such as the newest edition of *Guide Book of United States Coins* by R.S. Yeoman will illustrate or describe where to find the mint mark.

United States coins were minted at a number of different locations across the nation. Mint marks, mint locations, and inclusive dates are noted below:

U.S. COIN MINT MARKS, LOCATIONS, AND DATES

Mint Mark	Mint Location	Inclusive Dates
C	Charlotte, N.C.	1838–61
CC	Carson City, NV	1870–93
D	Dahlonega, GA	1838–61
D	Denver, CO	1906–Present
O	New Orleans, LA	1838–1909
P	Philadelphia, PA	1793–Present
no mint mark	Philadelphia, PA	1793–Present
S	San Francisco, CA	1864–Present

Mintage figures give an indication of the coin's potential value. The fewer coins minted the more the laws of supply and demand can drive up prices. Other factors also come into play. Large numbers of coins have been melted down over the years and significant quantities of other coins are effectively out of circulation in collections and bank vaults, thereby, at least temporarily, impacting demand and supply levels.

Coin condition plays a large role in valuation and pricing of collector coins. Methods of manufacturing coins include proof strike (coins not intended for general circulation), business strike coins (uncirculated or mint state coins never spent), and circulated (coins which entered general circulation and consequently show signs of wear such as scratches, worn edges, etc.).

To help in deciphering coin condition and aid in valuation, the American Numismatic Association (ANA) established the following grading system:

MS-70:   **Perfect Uncirculated.** Coins in a pristine condition. An estimated two percent of all uncirculated coins garner this rare rating.

MS-65:   **Choice Brilliant Uncirculated.** Coins with a minimum number of contact marks indicating a good mint strike. Between five and ten percent of all uncirculated coins earn this designation.

MS-60:   **Uncirculated.** May have heavy marks in all areas. This represents the final level of investment quality coins. Coins below this grading level should be considered for numismatic purposes only.

AU-55:   **Choice About Uncirculated.** Coins exhibiting minimal wear due to circulation.

AU-50:   **About Uncirculated.** Traces of wear on nearly all of the highest areas

EF-45:   **Choice Extremely Fine.** Light overall wear on highest points. All design details very sharp.

EF-40:   **Extremely Fine.** Only slight wear but more extensive than EF-45.

VF-30:   **Choice Very Fine.** Light even wear on the surface. All lettering and major features sharp.

VF-20:   **Very Fine.** Moderate wear on highest parts.

F-12:   **Fine.** Moderate to considerable even wear. All lettering visible but with some weakness.

VG-8:   **Very Good.** Well worn with fine details worn nearly smooth.

G-4:   **Good.** Heavily worn with major features visible in outline form but without center detail.

In addition, some coin dealers have added intermediate grades to distinguish between coins between two levels on the ANA grading scale.

Dealing with a reputable dealer and taking advantage of certified coin grading offers protection, but the best way to insure you get what you pay for is to learn how to grade coins yourself. This takes time and practice.

Keeping informed on coin prices and coin trends also pays off in the long run. Subscribe to a monthly coin magazine and regularly review current copies of coin price digests.

Consider coin investing with a long-term perspective. Search for coins with an uninterrupted track record of rising prices over a period of years. Make sure to compare prices and purchase only from coin dealers who will provide a written 10-day return privilege and written grading guaranty. For more expensive purchases, it's wise to have the coin appraised by a reputable third party to ascertain its proper grading and value.

As with your other investments, you need to diversify your coin portfolio. Auctions and estate sales often deliver investment quality coins at below market prices if you keep a sharp eye out for such events.

Here's a sample of Blanchard and Company coin recommendations made during July 1993.

BLANCHARD GOLD COIN RECOMMENDATIONS

COIN Description	Grade	7-6-93 Ask Price	72 Mo. High Bid Price	72 Mo. Low Bid Price
$2.50 Ind Qr Eag	MS63	$1,231	$2,078	$ 482
$5 Ind Hf Eagle	MS63	3,065	5,750	2,166
$10 Indian Eagle	MS63	1,461	2,711	808
$20 Lib Dbl Eagle	MS64	1,637	4,607	1,158

Caveat Emptor (Buyer Beware)

"Be extremely careful when purchasing esoteric gold coins. For example, California Fractional Gold coins struck between 1852–

1882, as a result of the gold rush, are currently being sold for several thousands of dollars when in reality they are only worth several hundreds," advises Russell A. Augustin, director of numismatics for Blanchard and Company.

Gold Mining Companies

Moving closer to the supply of the glittering metal, the shares of gold mining stocks offer the opportunity to hedge with gold and prosper with the good fortunes of well-managed mining companies.

Of course, it's important to recognize that mining company stocks do not represent pure gold plays. Many gold mining firms also have other operations that are not directly impacted by the forces that move gold prices. In addition, the companies themselves and the market price of their stocks are impacted by factors outside of the gold realm.

For instance, swings in the stock market, changing interest rates, natural disasters, equipment breakdowns, management decisions, etc., all impact the price of a gold mining company's stock price while not necessarily affecting the price of gold.

There are a number of well-run gold mining companies throughout the world. This allows you to geographically diversify your gold portfolio.

For the conservative investor, it's wise to stick with the proven, major producers with known reserves and an active exploration program and the financial assets to pursue unique competitive market opportunities as they arise.

Liquidity and ease of investing rank as major reasons to consider gold mining stocks. There are no storage, insurance, and delivery charges. You don't have to worry about changing investor sentiment for a particular mint mark or date or grade quality deterioration by exposure to the elements or improper handling.

Shares of South African gold mining companies, the world's largest gold producer, trade on United States stock exchanges as ADRs (refer back to Chapter Two, for a discussion of American

Depositary Receipts). Major South African gold producers include Anglo American Corporation of South Africa (OTC: ANGLY), Blyvooruitzicht Gold Mining Company OTC: BLYVY), De Beers Consolidated Mines, Limited (OTC: DBRSY), Driefontein Consolidated, Ltd. (OTC: DRFNY), Free State Consolidated Gold Mines, Ltd. (OTC: FSCNY), Kloof Gold Mining Company, Ltd. (OTC: KLOFY), and Western Deep Levels, Ltd. (OTC: WDEPY).

North American gold mining producers include United States based-Homestake Mining Company (NYSE: HM), Newmont Mining Corporation (NYSE: NEM), Pegasus Gold, Inc. (ASE: PGU), as well as Canadian-based American Barrick Resources Corporation (NYSE: ABX), Echo Bay Mines, Ltd., (ASE: ECO), Lac Minerals, Ltd. (NYSE: LAC), Placer Dome, Inc.(NYSE: PDG), and Teck Corporation (TSE: TEKB.TO).

One gold mining company that bears watching is Spokane, Washington-headquartered Pegasus Gold, Inc. (ASE: PGU). A medium-sized producer (1992 production 382,100 ounces), Pegasus operates production facilities in Idaho, Montana, and Nevada using both conventional open-pit mining and milling techniques as well as the innovative heap leaching gold extracting process.

The company runs an active exporation and acquisition program that promises to boost production levels in excess of 75 percent to 700,000 ounces in the next few years. Pegasus sports a wealth of cash reserves with over $90 million in its coffers and a minimal $36 million in long-term debt. With a cash cost around $230 per ounce, the company expects to generate over $1.10 per share in cash flow in 1993 and around $1.50 per share in 1994.

For 1993, Pegasus looks to make approximately 30 cents per share. However, the firm's long-term potential with production capacity of 700,000 ounces and a surge in gold prices above the $400 level could cause Pegasus' stock price to soar. See Figure 5–5, Pegasus Gold, Inc. Stock Price Chart.

Canadian American Barrick Resources Corporation (NYSE: ABX) represents another unique gold mining situation. A boost in gold production, cost cutting measures and a successful hedging program combined to create record profits for American Barrick

Figure 5–5
PEGASUS GOLD INC. STOCK PRICE CHART

PEGASUS GOLD INC. ASE-PGU | RECENT PRICE **26** | P/E RATIO **65.0** (Trailing: 83.9 / Median: NMF) | RELATIVE P/E RATIO **4.09** | DIV'D YLD **0.4%** | VALUE LINE **1228**

| TIMELINESS **3** Average | High: | 14.0 | 10.3 | 11.3 | 26.4 | 17.3 | 15.4 | 16.1 | 14.1 | 18.5 | 27.6 |
| (Relative Price Performance Next 12 Mos.) | Low: | 5.9 | 5.3 | 5.4 | 10.8 | 10.8 | 8.9 | 9.1 | 9.6 | 11.4 | 12.6 |

SAFETY **3** Average (Scale: 1 Highest to 5 Lowest)
BETA .10 (1.00 = Market)

1996-98 PROJECTIONS
	Price	Gain	Ann'l Total Return
High	35	(+35%)	9%
Low	25	(-5%)	Nil

Insider Decisions
	A	S	O	N	D	J	F	M	A
to Buy	0	0	0	0	0	0	0	0	0
Options	0	0	0	0	0	0	0	1	0
to Sell	0	0	0	0	0	0	1	0	0

Institutional Decisions
	3Q92	4Q92	1Q93
to Buy	23	32	30
to Sell	32	21	18
Hld's(000)	11491	13000	13109

Percent 18.0 / 12.0 / 6.0 shares traded

CAPITAL STRUCTURE as of 6/30/93
Total Debt $51.0 mill. Due in 5 Yrs $51.0 mill.
LT Debt $45.2 mill. LT Interest $2.8 mill.

(Total interest coverage: 4.4x)   (12% of Cap'l)

Pension Liability None

Pfd Stock None

Common Stock 33,460,003 shs.   (88% of Cap'l)

	1977	1978	1979	1980	1981	1982	1983	1984	1985	1986	1987	1988	1989	1990	1991	1992	1993	1994	© VALUE LINE PUB., INC.	96-98
	--	--	--	--	--	--	--	3.72	1.53	2.34	4.70	6.81	7.39	6.87	5.61	5.79	**5.95**	**6.80**	Sales per sh	*10.20*
	--	--	--	--	--	--	--	.36	d.08	.65	1.27	1.53	1.41	1.44	1.19	1.24	**1.30**	**1.60**	"Cash Flow" per sh	*2.65*
	--	--	--	--	--	--	--	.33	d.11	.35	.70	.66	.41	.43	.37	.38	**.40**	**.55**	Earnings per sh A	*1.20*
	--	--	--	--	--	--	--	--	--	--	.10	.10	.10	.10	.10	.10	**.10**	**.15**	Div'ds Decl'd per sh B	*.30*
	--	--	--	--	--	--	--	1.19	1.49	4.44	1.45	1.45	1.51	2.28	1.39	.89	**.50**	**1.20**	Cap'l Spending per sh	*1.60*
	--	--	--	--	--	--	--	5.05	4.26	4.87	8.66	9.29	9.66	8.04	8.82	9.31	**9.10**	**9.80**	Book Value per sh	*12.25*
	--	--	--	--	--	--	--	8.93	11.80	14.95	23.51	23.89	24.15	24.70	27.86	31.47	**33.50**	**33.70**	Common Shs Outst'g C	*34.30*
	--	--	--	--	--	--	--	28.3	--	21.2	26.6	19.9	27.5	27.1	32.4	37.2	*Bold figures are*		Avg Ann'l P/E Ratio	*26.0*
	--	--	--	--	--	--	--	2.64	--	1.44	1.78	1.65	2.08	2.01	2.07	2.25	*Value Line estimates*		Relative P/E Ratio	*2.00*
	--	--	--	--	--	--	--	--	--	.5%	.8%	.9%	.9%	.9%	.8%	.7%			Avg Ann'l Div'd Yield	*1.0%*
	--	--	--	--	--	--	--	33.3	18.0	35.1	110.4	162.8	178.4	169.6	156.2	182.2	**200**	**230**	Sales ($mill)	*350*
	--	--	--	--	--	--	--	4.5%	NMF	26.4%	27.2%	21.5%	23.5%	22.6%	23.3%	22.9%	**23.5%**	**25.0%**	Operating Margin	*28.0%*
	--	--	--	--	--	--	--	.4	.3	5.1	15.3	20.9	24.3	25.0	23.5	27.8	**30.0**	**35.0**	Depreciation ($mill)	*50.0*
	--	--	--	--	--	--	--	2.9	d1.2	4.7	14.5	15.6	9.8	10.5	9.6	11.2	**13.0**	**18.5**	Net Profit ($mill)	*41.0*
	--	--	--	--	--	--	--	--	--	--	16.8%	28.8%	35.7%	23.2%	9.5%	12.8%	**18.0%**	**20.0%**	Income Tax Rate	*20.0%*
	--	--	--	--	--	--	--	8.6%	NMF	13.3%	13.1%	9.6%	5.5%	6.2%	6.1%	6.2%	**6.5%**	**8.0%**	Net Profit Margin	*11.7%*
	--	--	--	--	--	--	--	18.2	29.7	37.7	88.0	76.1	45.2	42.1	96.2	124.6	**145**		Working Cap'l ($mill)	*210*
	--	--	--	--	--	--	--	.2	23.5	79.0	36.3	33.4	32.1	48.2	65.4	41.8	**25.0**	**25.0**	Long-Term Debt ($mill)	*25.0*
	--	--	--	--	--	--	--	45.1	50.3	72.7	203.6	221.9	233.2	198.5	245.7	293.1	**305**	**330**	Net Worth ($mill)	*420*
	--	--	--	--	--	--	--	6.6%	NMF	3.7%	7.1%	6.9%	4.2%	5.2%	3.9%	3.9%	**4.5%**	**5.5%**	% Earned Total Cap'l	*9.5%*
	--	--	--	--	--	--	--	6.3%	NMF	6.4%	7.1%	7.0%	4.2%	5.3%	3.9%	3.9%	**4.5%**	**5.5%**	% Earned Net Worth	*10.0%*
	--	--	--	--	--	--	--	6.3%	NMF	6.4%	6.0%	6.0%	3.2%	4.1%	2.9%	2.9%	**3.0%**	**4.0%**	% Retained to Comm Eq	*7.0%*
	--	--	--	--	--	--	--	--	--	16%	15%	24%	23%	26%	25%	26%	**27%**		% All Div'ds to Net Prof	*25%*

Relative Price Strength
Shaded areas indicate recessions
Options: CBOE, TCO

BUSINESS: Pegasus Gold Inc. produces gold (1992 output 382,100 oz.), silver (2.12 million oz.), lead (7,200 tons), and zinc (19,400 tons), using open-pit mining methods, heap leaching technology, and conventional milling practices. Operates the Zortman/Landusky, Montana Tunnels and Beal Mountain in Montana; the Florida Canyon and Relief Canyon mines in Nevada; and the Black Pine mine in Idaho. Has 61% interest in Zapopan NL in Australia; 32.3% int. in USMX. 1992 depr. rate: 8.8%. Has about .654 empls., 4,600 shrhldrs. Fidelity Management owns 7.6% of common; Van Eck Mgt., 5.4%; Insiders, about 1.0% (4/93 Proxy). Pres. & C.E.O.: Werner G. Nennecker. Inc.: BC, Canada. Addr.: North 9 Post, Suite 400, Spokane, Washington 99201. Tel.: 509-624-4653.

in 1992 and most likely again in 1993. When gold prices started pushing upward in 1993, the move helped the firm's stock price breakout of a consolidation pattern around the $24 per share level, after surging 60 percent from a low around $15 per share in early March, 1993. See Figure 5–6, American Barrick Resources Corporation Stock Price Chart.

Barrick's hedging program locks in an average price for its gold at $400 an ounce and as gold rises above that level, the company stands ready to participate in price upswings with higher

Figure 5–6
AMERICAN BARRICK RESOURCES CORPORATION
STOCK PRICE CHART

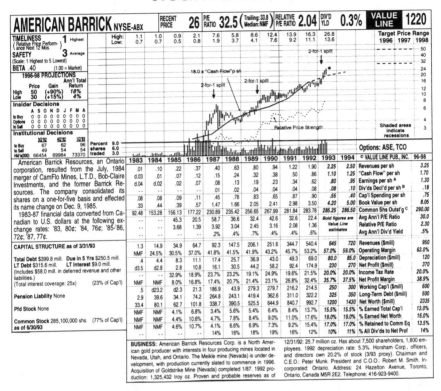

earnings. Earnings in 1992 surged 82 percent to 62 cents per share on a revenue rise of 45 percent to $554 million. No matter which way gold prices move, American Barrick should be covered. In mid-1993, the firms reported a 99 EPS ranking, the highest possible, from *Investor's Business Daily*.

Investing in gold mining stocks, just as investing in gold bullion, requires plenty of study. You can't just jump on the bandwagon because everybody else is doing it. Follow changes in gold prices and the reasons behind them. Don't make the mistake of joining in too late, only to purchase your stake at the peak. You want to join the ride but not on the way down.

To be a successful gold investor, you need to keep appraised of economic conditions, political crisis hot-spots, production capacity (current and potential), possible changes in demand and supply conditions, and investor sentiment.

For those investors with a more speculative bent, you could try trading gold company shares for short-term profits. That's exactly what I did with Benguet Corporation, a Philippine gold mining company, back in the 1980s when gold prices went sky high and were quite volatile.

Granted, the Benguet trading pattern does not occur with regular frequency but the example clearly illustrates a successful trading strategy. As you can see, if you keep a sharp eye out for these unique profit opportunities, you can boost your investment performance tremendously.

I first reported on the Benguet phenomenon back in November 1983, in an article for *Technical Analysis of Stocks and Commodities* and revisited Benguet in a follow-up article that appeared in the same investment journal in November 1985.

I had followed Benguet and the volatility of its stock price for a number of years, trading the stock on and off and making some nice profits. I then embarked on a strategy to earn a 36 percent gain on my Benguet transactions after commissions. I fully recognized that my profit goals probably wouldn't be realized, but I also felt with some proper timing, a watchful eye, and a lot of luck, the plan was not entirely unrealistic.

To make a long story short, purchases and sales of Benguet stock for the period March 18, 1982, through April 11, 1983, yielded an annualized return exceeding 163 percent. Even more important, if I had purchased Benguet stock at the beginning of that time period and held onto it until the end instead of actively trading, I would have earned an annualized return of 107 percent.

Now, nobody would kick a 107 percent return in the teeth but that buy and hold strategy performance under-performed my trading tactic by 56 percent.

Although Benguet traded in a relatively narrow price range over the course of a year, it exhibited some wide price swings on a monthly, weekly, and even daily basis. This allowed a close observer of the stock's volatility ample opportunity to buy and sell the stock numerous times during the year, earning incremental profits that helped creep toward the goal of extraordinary gains.

To get a feel for the strategy assume the following goal of earning a return of 36 percent for the year.

Investment Amount:	$4,000
Average Share Purchase:	500 shares @ $8 per share
Investment Goal:	36%; $4,000 x .36 = $1,440
Goal per month:	3% (36/12), assuming one round trip trade per month

Based on the assumption of one sale per month, the following figures apply to each month's anticipated trade.

Investment	$4,000
Purchase Commission	55
Sale Commission	60
Profit Objective ($4,000 x .03)	120
Gross Amount needed per trade	$4,235
Sales Price Needed to Achieve Investment Goal (4,235/500)	$8.50 per share

In other words, a 50 cent price swing was required each month to achieve a 36 percent annual return.

The strategy was to purchase Benguet stock at least 12 times during the year and sell each time its price rose a half a point or 50 cents per share. This would earn a return of $1,620 or 40 percent after commissions. At an average of one trade per month, I anticipated some months with no trades and other months with several trades occurring.

That, in fact, was how it turned out. I made multiple purchases in September, January, and February and multiple sales in July, September, December, and April. Of the 15 trades, 14 were profitable and one turned into a loss situation. Using limit and stop loss orders helped make sure market moves were not missed and limited downside risk.

Investing in a low priced stock like Benguet permits the investor to purchase enough shares to let a half point price swing make a big difference in investment returns after commissions.

Studying Benguet stock price movements indicated it had a support level of $4 per share on the downside and $12 per share on the upside. See Figure 5–7, Benguet Trendline.

Table 5–3 shows Benguet trades including transactions with percentage gains ranging from less than 6 percent to over 21 percent.

The average investment per trade amounted to $2,432 and the total gain of $3,971 delivered an average annual return of 163.28 percent (3,971/2,432).

While some of the trades earned less than $200 and under a six percent gain, the ownership time frame allowed a rapid in-

Figure 5–7
BENGUET CORPORATION TRENDLINE

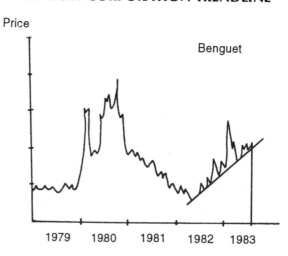

Price

Benguet

1979   1980   1981   1982   1983

Table 5–3
TABLE OF BENGUET TRADES
MARCH 8, 1982–APRIL 11, 1983

Benguet Corporation
NYSE: BE

Purchase Date	Sale Date	# of Shares	Amount Invested	Amount of Gain	Percent Gain/(Loss)
3/18/82	4/14/82	500	$1,908	$300	15.72%
5/07/82	7/21/82	800	3,170	370	11.67
5/17/82	7/21/82	900	3,553	432	12.15
8/06/82	8/20/82	500	1,920	410	21.35
9/01/82	9/03/82	600	2,977	642	21.56
9/01/82	9/03/82	400	1,990	415	20.85
9/21/82	10/11/82	400	2,343	158	6.74
9/27/82	12/21/82	200	1,105	138	12.48
12/17/82	12/29/82	500	3,115	330	10.59
1/06/83	1/06/83	400	3,445	187	5.41
1/24/83	2/01/83	300	2,791	261	9.35
2/14/83	3/09/83	100	1,050	(100)	(9.52)
2/28/83	4/11/83	200	1,585	91	5.74
2/28/83	4/11/83	400	3,154	190	6.02
3/21/83	4/11/83	300	2,368	147	6.20

vestment turnover. For example, the trade on January 6, 1983 lasted only two hours from purchase to sale.

In deciding whether or not a particular stock represents a good trading candidate, it's essential to know its past price pattern and current price swings. It's helpful to chart the price movements daily.

For a comprehensive discussion of resistance levels, support levels, trendlines, trading gaps, and other technical analysis techniques, pick up a copy of my book, *Divining the Dow* (Probus, 1993), a Fortune Book Club selection in August 1993.

Figure 5–8, Daily Price Chart, Figure 5–9, Support Level, and Figure 5–10, Resistance Level illustrate some simple charting techniques which could be put to use in tracking stock price movements.

Figure 5–8
DAILY PRICE CHART

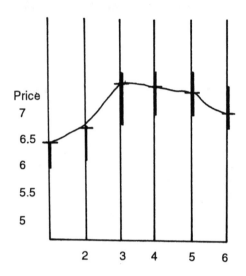

Figure 5–9
SUPPORT LEVEL

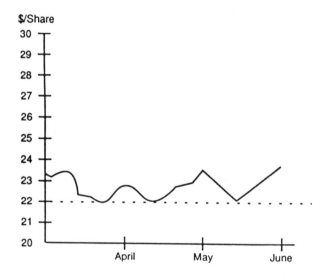

Figure 5–10
RESISTANCE LEVEL

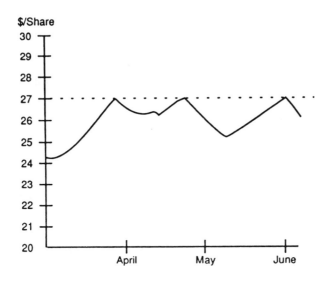

The follow-up November, 1985 article covered trades after the April 1983 period. While Benguet's wild price fluctuations tended to taper off as gold prices moved off historic highs, it still moved enough to generate a better than 62 percent return during the year from May 1983 to June 1984.

Search out stocks that can deliver above average returns under unique circumstances. Gold mining company stocks fall into this category during periods of uncertain economic and political environments.

Gold Mutual Funds

If picking individual gold mining stocks has you baffled, you can opt for the mutual fund approach. There's a bevy of mutual funds specializing in the gold stock arena, and sometimes investing in other precious metals as well.

While some mutual funds concentrate their investments in gold mining company stocks, others combine their stock positions with purchases of gold bullion, hopefully, giving their investors the best of both worlds. Others hedge their positions with both puts and calls.

If you choose to go the mutual fund route, you still need to perform some upfront investigative work. Find out the mix of portfolio assets (stocks, bullion, etc.) as well as determine the geographical location of the majority of assets. Does the mutual fund weight its portfolio heavily toward South African gold mining companies, with a degree of political risk, or is its asset mix more balanced geographically?

Of course, the mutual fund approach avoids the headaches of dealing with delivery, storage, assaying, and insuring of gold bullion or gold coins.

Lexington Strategic Investments Fund, which invests in South African gold mining companies, earned a whopping 82.5 percent return for the one year period ended June 30, 1993. However, the fund's five year return comes in at a negative 23.1 percent.

Taking a more balanced approach, United Services World Gold Fund delivered positive performances for both the one-year and five-year time frames, 53.7 percent and 5.0 percent respectively.

The list of gold mutual funds in Table 5–4 will give you plenty of food for thought.

There are a lot of political and economic unknowns out there. For example, what is the future of Yeltsin and Russia and how will that impact world financial markets? In addition, early signs of inflation are beginning to crop up. President Clinton's economic plan could backfire and plunge the country deep into recession. All of these scenarios point to reasons why investors should consider adding gold as a hedge to their portfolio.

One way to keep appraised of the direction of gold prices and gold investments is to subscribe to one or two of the many gold investment newsletters.

Table 5–4
GOLD MUTUAL FUNDS

Fund	Telephone Number
Benham Gold Equities Index	800-472-3389
Blanchard Precious Metals	800-922-7771
Bull & Bear Gold Investors	800-847-4200
Dean Witter Precious Metals	800-869-3863
Enterprise Precious Metals	800-432-4320
Excel Midas Gold Shares	800-783-3444
Fidelity Select-American Gold	800-544-8888
Fidelity Select Precious Metals	800-544-8888
Financial Portfolio: Gold	800-525-8085
Franklin Gold	800-342-5236
J. Hancock FR Gold & Gov A & B	800-225-5291
IDS Precious Metals	800-328-8300
Keystone Precious Metals	800-343-2898
Lexington Goldfund	800-526-0056
Lexington Strategic Investments Fund	800-526-0056
Mainstay: Gold & Precious Metals	800-522-4202
MFS Lifetime Gold & Natural	800-225-2606
Monitrend Gold	800-251-1970
Oppenheimer Gold & Sp Minerals	800-525-7048
Pioneer Growth Gold Shares	800-225-6292
Rushmore Precious Metals Index	800-343-3355
Scudder Gold	800-225-2470
Thompson Precious Metals A & B	800-227-7337
United Gold & Gov	800-366-5465
U.S. Gold Shares	800-873-8637

The Dines Letter has been published since January 1960 by James Dines, often called the "original gold bug." In a May 18, 1992 article for Barron's, Dines talked about many gold technical indicators registering a deep "over-sold" condition. His timing was just right since the article appeared just before the gold market bottomed out. An annual subscription to *The Dines Letter* costs $195 or you can try a two-month look-see for $49 or six-month trial for $115. To order, write to Box 22, Belvedere, California 94920 or call 800-845-8259.

The Value Line Investment Survey covers the major North American and South African gold mining companies and can be found at most libraries.

If you are looking for relatively unfollowed gold mining companies to discover, try J. Taylor's *Gold & Gold* Stocks newsletter. In addition to reporting on gold trends, Taylor profiles a bevy of North American gold mining companies you won't find in *Value Line*. His newsletter provides buy recommendations and can be ordered from P. O. Box 871, Woodside, New York 11377 or call 718-457-1426. An annual subscription runs $89.

Silver and Other Metals

Silver typically trades in the shadow of its more valuable cousin, gold. Like gold, silver is used in a number of industrial processes from film manufacturing to electronic products. In addition, silverware and jewelry create demand for silver.

In mid-1993, silver traded around $4.60 per ounce, a far cry from the $50 per ounce the metal commanded during the heady speculative days in early 1980.

The silver investor can purchase silver bars, coins or bags of coins. Silver certificates are also available. The basics of silver investing are comparable to gold investing and will not be repeated here.

One silver trading strategy consists of playing the gold/silver ratio. Under this tactic, when the cost of purchasing one ounce of gold in terms of selling silver ounces exceeds a certain ratio, then silver is considered to be undervalued in relation to gold. The lowest silver/gold ratio occurred in January 1980 when it narrowed to 17 ounces of silver to one ounce of gold. The largest ratio spread was around 90 to 1 silver to gold.

Naysayers contend that the silver/gold trading theory no longer works since silver and gold have gone their separate ways and no longer clearly relate to each other.

Both gold and silver can be invested in through the purchase of futures contracts. In essence, a futures contract is an agreement for the purchaser to buy and the seller to sell a specific amount of a commodity (gold or silver), at an agreed price on a specified date in the future.

For information on gold and silver production, prices, reserves, etc., The Gold Institute and The Silver Institute in Washington, D.C. publish annual world surveys on both metals as well as bimonthly newsletters on the metals. To request subscription information and prices, both are located at 1112 Sixteenth Street, Suite 240, Washington, D.C. 20036 or call 202-835-0185.

The same basic investing concepts work for other precious metals such as platinum and palladium. Again, some precious metals watchers advocate tracking the spread between gold prices and prices of other precious metals in search of market anomalies and profit opportunities.

6

options

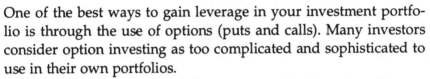

One of the best ways to gain leverage in your investment portfolio is through the use of options (puts and calls). Many investors consider option investing as too complicated and sophisticated to use in their own portfolios.

Thomas Dorsey, president of Dorsey, Wright & Associates, a Richmond, Virginia investment risk management firm specializing in point and figure analysis of equities and options, explains options this way.

"A lot of investors believe that investing in options is too speculative. I always ask investors at seminars to raise their hands if they have ever owned a put. When a few hands are raised and they look at each other confused, I then ask if they own a car now or have ever owned a car. Of course, most people raise their hands. I then inform them that they have already invested in a put option because that is exactly how an automobile insurance policy works. You pay a premium and the insurance company agrees to purchase your car (or repair it) at a future date if you have an accident. See, options are not as foreign to most investors as first thought," says Dorsey.

Exactly what is an option? An option is a security which provides the right to purchase or sell a specified number of shares of a particular stock at a fixed price for a specified time period. There are two kinds of options, calls and puts.

A call option gives the buyer the right to purchase 100 shares of a particular stock at an agreed upon price for a specific period of time. On the other hand, a put option gives the investor the right to sell 100 shares of a specified stock for an agreed upon price for a set period of time.

If the option is not sold or exercised prior to the expiration date, the option expires worthless and all monies paid for the option are forfeited.

There are several reasons investors use options.

First of all, options can be purchased for a fraction of the per share cost of stock, thus offering the possibility of substantially increasing investment return through leverage. Second, the proper use of options can limit investment risk. Since the worst that can happen is that the option expires worthless, the investor's risk is limited to the cost of the option premium. Third, options can be used as insurance to protect gains or limit potential losses. Finally, you can earn extra income on stock you own and thus enhance your overall investment return by writing (selling) call options.

In order to trade options, you will need to open an option account. In essence, that involves signing an option agreement with your broker signifying that you agree to abide by the option trading rules and regulations. Make sure you thoroughly read and understand what you are signing.

Ask your broker for a copy of *Characteristics and Risks of Standardized Options* published by The American Stock Exchange. This publication helps the investor understand how stock options work. You can also request a copy directly from the American Stock Exchange by sending a request to 86 Trinity Place, New York, New York 10006.

Options are traded on five exchanges as follows:

American Stock Exchange
Chicago Board of Options
New York Stock Exchange
Pacific Stock Exchange
Philadelphia Stock Exchange

In addition, the five exchanges are members of the Options Clearing Corporation, formed to ensure proper execution of option trades for options listed on the above exchanges.

Options trade at various exercise price intervals based on the stock price. For example, stocks trading between $5 to $25 per share usually have options with price intervals of $2 1/2 points, stocks trading in the $25-$200 price range have options with price intervals of five points, and stocks trading above $200 per share have options with 10 point price intervals.

OPTION CASE STUDIES

Now, let's take a look at some examples illustrating how options actually work and how they can improve your investment performance.

Call Options

Call options are purchased with the anticipation that the price of the underlying stock will rise in value in excess of the premium paid for the call. When this happens, the call option holder can sell the call for a higher price and pocket the profit on the transaction or exercise the right to purchase the shares of stock at the exercise price and hold the stock.

The call prices listed in the financial pages represent the price to purchase one share of common stock. Since options are traded in units with rights to 100 shares of stock, multiply the listed option price by 100 to arrive at your cost to purchase an option for 100 shares of stock.

Assume you believe the shares of XYZ Corporation are going to rise but don't want to invest a large sum of money to earn your desired return. Instead of purchasing 500 shares at the current price of $50 per share for a total investment of $25,000 ($50 × 500), you purchase 50 options at $1 which gives you the right to purchase 5,000 shares of XYZ stock at $55 per share. Your option premium costs you $5,000 ($1 × 50 × 100). For one fifth of the investment, you control 10 times as many shares of common stock.

If the stock price rises $5 per share, the option premium could rise from $1 to $3. Your profit on the long position of holding the stock would amount to $2,500 ($5 × 500) or a 10 percent return on your investment. In comparison, your call option position would now be worth $15,000 ($3 × 50 × 100) and you would have earned a profit of $10,000, or a tripling of your original investment.

Now, if the stock continues to rise above the exercise price of the call option, the power of leverage really kicks in and the price advance of the option and your returns could skyrocket. For example, if the stock price rises to $60 per share and the option price surges to $7, your results change dramatically.

Under this scenario, your long position profit now totals $5,000 ($10 × 500) for a 20 percent return. However, if you were savvy enough to have taken the option route, you would have garnered a profit of $30,000 ($6 × 50 × 100) or six times your original investment.

Of course, such lucrative profit opportunities do not come without risks. If the stock price of XYZ, Inc. failed to rise above the exercise price of $55 per share, your call option would have expired worthless and you would have suffered a $5,000 loss. With a long stock position, you could have even made money if the stock rose above the $50 per share purchase price.

Many factors enter into the price or premium of an option including the price of the underlying stock, the exercise price, the amount of time remaining till expiration of the option, interest rates, anticipated dividends, and the volatility of the market in general and the underlying security in particular.

For example, in the above case, if the remaining time to maturity were relatively long, the option could command a higher price if investors felt the stock price could rise higher. Likewise, if the time to maturity were very short, the option price might be more near the intrinsic value of the option (the difference between the stock market price and the exercise price or $5 ($60-$55) instead of $6 as indicated.

All of these factors must be considered when assessing your risk/reward posture.

Covered Call Strategies

The covered call writer sells a call option for a premium on a stock he or she owns in his or her portfolio. You will be required to deposit the shares in your account as collateral to guarantee your delivery of the stock in the event the call option holder decides to exercise the option and purchase the shares at the exercise price. You will continue to receive any dividends paid on your stock until the option is exercised.

Covered call strategies can be used to lock in gains already achieved, offset possible losses with a stock price downturn, and capitalize on additional investment returns by earning premiums while the market moves sideways. If the options expire unexercised, options can be sold for premiums again and again, substantially increasing investment gains.

Other benefits of writing covered calls include effectively purchasing the stock at a discount by writing a call option while simultaneously buying the security and increasing the yield on a security by combining dividend earnings with option premiums.

When writing a call option, you promise the buyer you will sell your shares of a particular security for a specified (exercise) price for a given period of time. In exchange, the buyer of the call option pays you a premium.

This transaction is called a "covered call" because you already own the stock and can "cover" the exercise of the option by delivering the shares. In contrast, writing a call option without owning the underlying security is termed writing a "naked" option.

Consider the information in Table 6–1 on ABC Corporation stock and options. That information can be found in the options tables of financial journals such as *Barron's*, *Investor's Business Daily*, and *The Wall Street Journal*.

Table 6–1
ABC CORPORATION STOCK AND OPTIONS

Option NY Close	Strike Price	Sept	Calls Oct	Jan
ABC	30	7 1/4	s	s
37 1/2	35	2 7/16	3 1/8	s
37 1/2	40	1/16	1/2	1 1/2
37 1/2	45	r	1/8	s

r denotes not traded
s denotes no option offered

Call Case Study #1

Assume you own 300 shares of ABC Corporation which you purchased at $30 per share. You write three September covered calls with an exercise or strike price of $30 per share and receive a total premium of $2,175 ($7.25 × 3 × 100). This protects your investment gain from the $30 per share at which you purchased your ABC shares to the current market price of $37 1/2 per share in case the stock starts to decline.

Call Case Study #2

To affect a discount in the price at which you purchase a stock, you can simultaneously write a call option. For example, assume you buy 300 shares of ABC stock at the current price of $37 1/2 per share and also wrote a January call with a strike price of $40 for 1 1/2. You will receive $450 ($1.50 × 3 × 100) in premiums, thereby resulting in a net cost of $10,800 ($11,250 − $450), a reduction in the cost of the shares of four percent (450/11,250).

Call Case Study #3

ABC's indicated dividend rate is $1.40 per share annually, resulting in a yield of 3.7 percent based on a purchase price of $37 1/2 per share. By writing covered calls on a regular basis, you can reasonably expect to raise your yield considerably. For instance, if you write covered calls four times a year and earn an average 13/16 in premium, your yield would rise to 12.4 percent on an annual basis.

Covered Call Drawbacks

The first and most obvious danger in writing covered calls lies in the prospect that the stock price may rise and the option holder may exercise the option and take ownership of your shares. If the exercise or strike price is $40 per share and the stock market price rises to $50 per share, you have forfeited your right to participate in any stock price rise above the $50 per share exercise price.

You also run the risk that the stock may fall more in value than you have earned in premiums by selling the covered call options.

Writing "Naked" Options

As mentioned earlier, writing an option without owning the underlying stock is termed writing "naked" options because you don't have the stock to backup delivery of the shares. In this instance, if the option holder exercises his or her right to purchase the shares, the option writer must either purchase the shares in the open market at prevailing prices in order to deliver the shares or make a closing purchase option transaction.

Obviously, writing naked options consists of taking a much higher risk posture than writing a covered call. While covered call writing entails risks, they are known and can be quantified in advance. This is not true of naked option writing. The dollar amount of loss is virtually unlimited. In essence, the risk of writing naked options is limited only by the time remaining to expiration of the option.

Brokerage firms require adequate collateral or margin from writers of naked options. As the price of the stock moves higher, you could be required to deliver additional collateral.

To be sure, naked option writing is not for the conservative investor.

Put Options

If you believe the price of a stock will fall in the future, you can use the purchase of put options to increase your profits and investment return.

The purchase of a put gives you the right to sell a particular stock at a specified price within a certain period of time. You will make money if the stock's market price declines because the value of the put will increase. Of course, the stock price must decrease in value in excess of the cost of the put option.

Another reason to buy a put is for insurance. Assume you like the stock price appreciation prospects of ABC Corporation but inherent weakness in the overall stock market brings more risk to the situation than you desire to undertake. In this case,

you could buy 100 shares of ABC at $40 per share and simultane-
ously purchase a put with an exercise price of $40 per share. If
the stock price increases, you participate in the upward movement with investment gains. Your only loss is the cost of the put
as it expires worthless.

However, if your concerns were right on target and the stock
price declined, then your put would kick in and offset the loss in
your long position of ABC stock. Depending on your comfort
level on the direction of the company's stock price, you could
purchase puts at prices different than what you pay for the common stock. This would reduce how much premium you pay for
the put but also increase your exposure to loss.

Just like their call counterparts, the price or premium commanded by puts varies in relation to changes in price of the underlying stock, time to expiration, interest rates, market and stock
price volatility, etc.

Consider the information in Table 6–2 on ABC stock and put
options:

Table 6–2
ABC STOCK AND PUT OPTIONS

Option NY Close	Strike Price	Oct	Puts Nov	Jan
ABC	35	1/8	1 1/16	s
37 1/2	40	2 3/4	3 1/8	s

s denotes no option offered

With a current market price of $37 1/2 per share for the
common stock, the put options with an exercise or strike price of
$40 per share are "in the money," meaning they already possess
intrinsic value because the put gives the holder the right to sell
the shares for a price higher than the current market price of the
ABC stock.

Puts can be effective in bearish markets or markets that exhibit a seesaw action providing opportunities to capitalize on downside thrusts.

Put Case Study #1

You already own 500 shares of ABC stock and still believe it should be a solid investment in the long run but you want to protect yourself against downside risk. A purchase of a put which will increase in value as the stock price decreases helps offset any losses incurred by downward pressure on ABC's stock price.

For example, your current holdings are worth $18,750 (500 shares at $37.50 per share). Assume you purchase 20 October puts with a strike price of $35 for a premium of 1/8 The premium will cost you $250 ($.125 × 20 × 100). A drop in the stock price to $34 per share before the October puts expire will result in a loss on your ABC stock holdings of $1,750 ($3.50 × 500), but a net gain of $1,750 [($1 × 2,000 shares) − $250 premium] on the put options results in an overall breakeven position.

Put Case Study #2

This time, assume that you believe that the ABC stock price will tumble from its current $37 1/2 per share level and close below $35 per share before the expiration of the November puts.

A purchase of 20 November puts with a strike price of $35 per share will cost you $1,375 ($.6875 × 20 × 100). This gives you the right to sell 2,000 shares of ABC stock at $35 per share. A drop in the price of ABC stock to $33 per share before expiration of your November puts will result in a gain of $2,625 [($2 × 2,000) − $1,375 commission], more than tripling your original investment.

WRITING PUT CONTRACTS

In addition to purchasing puts, you can also write put options. Under this scenario, you obligate yourself for a specified time to purchase shares of the underlying stock at the strike price in exchange for the premium. Investors write put options to earn premium income when they believe the price of the underlying stock will remain steady within a narrow range or will rise during the life of the option.

Again, the brokerage firm requires that the writer of a put option deposit and maintain adequate margin funds to guarantee the stock can be purchased in the event the option holder exercises the right to sell the writer the stock.

The writer can close out the put position prior to the expiration date by purchasing an identical put at the current market price. This transaction has the effect of liquidating or terminating the obligation to purchase the stock and the person has a profit or loss depending on the difference between what he or she received as a premium for writing the put option and what he or she paid for the identical put.

Puts can be either written naked (when you have no position in the underlying stock) or as a way to cover or reduce the risk of having a short position in a stock. See Chapter Eight, Short Selling, for a discussion of short selling strategies. Since a short position already requires the investor to put up margin, a seller of a put option with a short position in the stock would not be required to deliver additional margin collateral to the brokerage firm.

The writer of a naked put possesses a positive opinion on the upward trend of a particular stock. If the stock's price stays above the exercise price of the put option, the stock will not have to be purchased and the entire premium from writing the put will be profit. If the stock price does fall below the exercise price and the put is exercised, forcing the writer to purchase the stock at a price higher than current market price, the writer may be in line for a loss if the price of the stock continues to drop.

However, proper analysis of the stock's prospects and over-all price direction should help to reduce this possibility. The drop may only be temporary. If so, the put writer can also earn a profit on the stock as its price rises above the purchase price. In essence, the put writer takes a calculated risk of being forced to purchase the stock at a price above market value in exchange for earning the put premium.

OPTION INFORMATION SOURCES

A variety of option investment newsletters and publications exist to aid the option investor in developing successful trading strategies and uncovering unique option investment opportunities.

Value Line Publishing, Inc. publishes *Value Line Options* 48 times per year at an annual subscription rate of $445. It contains a wealth of information on options including special situation alerts, company news, relative volatility of individual options, trends in option premium levels, and recommended selected options for covered call writing and other option strategies. In addition, the subscriber receives *The Value Line Guide to Option Strategies*. To order or request information contact Value Line Publishing, Inc. at 711 Third Avenue, New York, New York 10017-4064 or call 212-687-3965.

R.H.M Associates publishes *The R.H.M. Survey of Warrants, Options & Low-Price Stocks* at subscription rates of $280 for 50 issues a year or $150 per half-year. See Chapter Nine, Warrants, for a discussion of warrant investment strategies. You can contact R.H.M. at 172 Forest Avenue, Glen Cove, New York 11542 or call 516-759-2904.

The R.H.M. investment newsletter includes a discussion of stocks in the news as well as listings of best situated options. For example, the June 25, 1993 issue featured an April 2, 1993 recommendation of American Barrick Resources Corporation options which proved to be "a well-timed and profitable pick."

In early April, 1993, the American Barrick January 1995 17 1/2 calls could be purchased for $3.50 while the firm's common stock traded around $16 per share. With a renewed interest in gold in mid-1993, investors pushed up American Barrick's stock price 38 percent or $6 to around $22 per share. In comparison, the call options shot up 134 percent to $8.18. Obviously, the leverage of options can substantially improve investment performance. See Chapter Five, Minding Metals, for a more detailed discussion of the prospects for American Barrick Resources Corporation.

LEAPS (Long-Term Equity Participation Securities)

The above American Barricks option example leads us to LEAPS, (long-term equity participation securities). Up until now, we have been evaluating stock options with maturities extending out a matter of months. In contrast, LEAPS are relatively new long-term options that reduce the risks of option investing by extending the time factor from months to up to two years.

Along with the new option security comes new investment strategies to reduce risk and improve return. For example, a conservative approach combines the purchase of LEAPS with a purchase of low-risk U.S. Treasuries. In theory, the strategy delivers a value gain if the stock rises and provides a cushion in the event the stock price declines. One approach recommends a 90/10 split, that is 90 percent invested in Treasuries and 10 percent invested in LEAPS. Even if the option expired worthless, your loss would only be the difference between the option premium and the income earned on the Treasuries. The right combination could deliver a breakeven or near breakeven situation even if the LEAPS expired worthless.

If all things go as planned and the price of the underlying stock rises, the LEAPS investor could earn both interest on the Treasuries and a capital gain on the rise in the value of the option.

Some caveats are in order. First of all, as new securities, LEAPS are still thinly traded. The use of "limit orders" is highly recommended in order to obtain the prices you want when you buy and sell these securities. Second, combining LEAPS with interest-earning securities involves a degree of market interest rate risk which can negatively impact the value of the interest-bearing security.

Another LEAPS investment strategy involves what is called a "hedge wrapper." In this case, the investor sells a long-term call option with a strike price higher than the current price of the underlying stock and simultaneously purchases a LEAP with a strike price below the stock's current market price.

As a result, you gain protection against a drop in stock price from the put option which increases in value as the stock's market price falls below the put's strike price.

OTHER OPTION INVESTMENT STRATEGIES

There are myriad ways to invest in options. As you gain more experience, you can investigate more sophisticated option strategies such as bull and bear spreads, ratio spreads, time spreads, straddles, and strategy combinations.

In addition to options on stocks, a number of other option alternatives exist. For instance, you can purchase options on currency, precious metals such as gold and silver, interest rate instruments or interest indexes such as the Long-Term Interest Rate index (LTX), and other indexes such as the Standard & Poor's (S&P) 500 Index. There are also a number of sector options available.

"Options represent a flexible risk management tool that more investors need to investigate," says Dorsey.

Dorsey uses two guiding principles in his option investing strategies. First, he recommends purchasing well in-the-money calls or puts with a few months remaining to expiration. He's convinced that being correct on the direction of individual stocks is possible. However, if the investor purchases out-of-the-money options, he or she must be correct on timing, the amount the stock will rise, and direction.

The second Dorsey principle lies in basing his recommendations on point-and-figure technical work versus trying to forecast the economy or company earnings. In addition to charts on stocks and indexes, Dorsey uses the NYSE Bullish Percent, created by the Chartcraft organization decades ago.

The NYSE Bullish Percent uses the sum of all NYSE stocks that point-and-figure analysis defines as bullish divided by the total number of NYSE listed stocks. According to Dorsey, the indicator's best signals occur when the Bullish Percent rises above 70 or drops below 30 and then reverses by six or more percentage points.

Options can greatly enhance your investment performance. Investigate the opportunities and risks, do your homework, and proceed cautiously as you should with any investment alternative.

7

preferreds

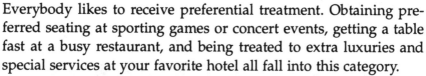

Everybody likes to receive preferential treatment. Obtaining preferred seating at sporting games or concert events, getting a table fast at a busy restaurant, and being treated to extra luxuries and special services at your favorite hotel all fall into this category.

However, you can obtain preferential treatment as an investor. A number of companies issue preferred stock which comes complete with special privileges for its owners.

Why do firms issue preferred stock? The major reason to offer preferred stock is to attract a different type of investor while raising capital. While the common shareholders are mainly concerned with capital appreciation, the preferred stock investor searches for current income.

Investors find preferred stock attractive because it provides a protected stream of income plus more safety of principal than offered by common stock. Like convertibles, preferreds are hybrid securities, a cross between common stocks and bonds. They deliver equity ownership in the company with some voting powers, but since they pay a stated rate of return in the form of a fixed dividend, they also resemble bonds.

One part of the preferential treatment lies in the fact that preferred stockholders are guaranteed that they receive their dividends before any dividends are paid on the common stock.

In addition to the dividend preferential treatment, the preferred stock also maintains a higher ranking in the ownership status of the company. In the event of the company's liquidation or bankruptcy, preferred stockholders possess a prior claim to company assets over common stockholders but behind that of bondholders.

In order to gain these preferences, preferred shareholders give up a few rights. First of all, their participation in management of the company is limited by restricted voting rights, their return is fixed by the stated dividend rate while common stock dividends can be raised periodically by board of director action, and their right to purchase new company securities may also be restricted.

CHARACTERISTICS OF PREFERRED STOCKS

Historically, preferred stock arose out of the numerous railroad bankruptcy reorganizations of the 1880's and 1890's. They appealed to conservative investors who desired stable but higher yields than offered by straight bonds, but not the risks associated with common stock ownership.

More recently, tax legislation made issuing preferreds very attractive to corporations. Under current tax law, companies holding preferred stock can exclude 70 percent of preferred dividend income from their federal income tax calculations. Due to this preferential tax advantage, all other things being equal, preferred stock typically offers a more generous yield than bonds.

For the most part, preferred stock market prices react more to changes in market interest rates than to the stock market in general or the market price of the company's common stock. Since the preferred dividend rate and its yield are fixed once the preferred stock is purchased, investors must compare its yield with competing investment alternatives in terms of both yield and safety.

Of course, the underlying company's financial strength and operating performance do affect the preferred stock's market price; however, their impact is much less than that on the common stock price. Traditionally, due to their fixed income attributes, the stock prices of preferreds have traded in much narrower ranges than their common stock counterparts, thus providing less volatility and more safety of principal.

Some detractors contend that preferreds possess the least favorable aspects of stocks and bonds. They don't have top priority in the event of a bankruptcy nor do they fully share in the profits of a common stock price as the company's financial performance improves.

The main appeal of preferreds lies in their ability to deliver a generous yield compared to other investment alternatives, plus deliver a higher degree of principal safety in terms of low market price fluctuation and more protection than offered by common stocks.

If it's capital appreciation you are seeking at the expense of current income and principal safety, then preferreds are not for you. If you desire competitive yields and safety, then it's wise to take a look at preferred stocks.

One of the preferred market's biggest attractions is that so few people understand it. Imperfect investor knowledge creates an inefficient market and unique investment opportunities. Therefore, with a little research, overall returns of preferreds can exceed those of either bonds or common stocks.

Until recently, utilities were the largest issuers of preferred stock because it allowed them to raise capital for construction without negatively impacting their debt/equity ratios and debt costs. In the past three years, however, financial institutions have taken over as the biggest issuers of preferreds, primarily due to new federal primary capital requirements.

Examples of banks now issuing preferreds include Bank America Corporation, Chase Manhattan Corporation, Chemical

Banking Corporation, Citicorp, and Republic New York Corporation.

The ability of preferreds to protect a corporation's debt rating and allow them to raise additional capital also attracted the industrial world. Since the end of 1991, General Motors Corporation, Ford Motor Company, and International Business Machines Corporation (IBM) created the three largest issues of corporate preferred stock on the market with 44 million shares or more each.

Another benefit to the issuer, preferred stock dividend payments are issued on an after-tax basis, versus bond interest payments which constitute a pre-tax expense.

The world of preferred investments continues to undergo change. A proliferation of adjustable rate preferreds promise investors some degree of protection against interest rate risk.

"Adjustable rate preferreds could catch on as an investment vehicle, particularly as the current low interest rate environment changes and interest rates start to rise with an economic recovery," says Gary Bice, vice president investments with Prudential Securities in Bloomfield Hills, Michigan.

It works like this, the adjustable rate preferred dividend payment is pegged to a composite interest index comprised of a variety of rates such as the three-month, one-year, and 10-year Treasury interest rates and adjusted periodically to reflect changes in that composite. Each adjustable preferred stock may carry its own unique way of computing just how the rate will be revised; so pay close attention to the composite and any factors entering into the calculation process. There may also be minimum and maximum dividend payments prescribed for the issue.

For example, The Republic New York Corporation $3.25 adjustable preferred stock calculates its adjustment using the highest of the three month, 10 year, or 20 year Treasury rates minus 160 basis points. The preferred stock dividend adjusts when the 30 year Treasury yield rises above 7.80 percent. It also includes a dividend floor of $3.25 and a dividend ceiling of $6.25 per share.

Under these terms, the preferred investor is guaranteed his or her dividend payment will not fall below the $3.25 per share level and can participate in interest rate rises at least up to the $6.25 per share preferred dividend level.

Adjustable rate provisions protect the investor against a decrease in the preferred stock market price, since they allow the investor to earn a higher yield as interest rates rise.

There's another way for preferred stockholders to share in higher dividends. The participating preferred stock receives a specified dividend but also has the right to share in any excess earnings which would normally go to the common stockholders.

Participation can take several forms. To illustrate, a $7 preferred stock could receive its stated dividend of $7 per share and then participate equally in a $2 per share payment to shareholders of both common stock and preferred stock. Under another scenario, the $7 preferred stockholder would first receive his or her $7 per share dividend payment, the common stock holder would receive a like amount and then both preferred and common stockholders would participate equally in any additional dividend payment.

Some preferred stock issues contain a cumulative clause allowing dividends to accumulate if dividend pay-outs are suspended during tough financial times. These accumulated dividends will have to be paid out to preferred shareholders before any dividends can be paid on the common stock when the company's economic fortunes turn around.

As indicated in Chapter Three, Captivating Convertibles, there's a link between convertibles and preferred securities called the convertible preferred. Just like its convertible bond counterpart, the convertible preferred stock carries a provision allowing the shareholder to convert his or her holdings into a certain number of common shares of the company at a specified price.

The convertible preferred offers the best of both worlds. It delivers an attractive yield combined with the added kicker of allowing the investor to participate in the upside move of the underlying common stock through its convertibility feature. Refer to the discussion in Chapter Three for how convertibles work.

To make their preferred stocks even more attractive to prospective investors, companies have added a number of other provisions such as protection against dilution by future bond or other preferred stock issues with greater rights and in the event of takeovers. Other provisions call for sinking funds to help ensure payoff of the preferred issue and minimum working capital requirements which have to be maintained to bolster preferred dividend paying capabilities.

Typically, preferred stock has a designated par value and fixed dividend rate, no maturity date and, if applicable, a conversion rate. The dividend may be expressed as either a stated dollar amount or as a percentage of the par value. For example, a preferred stock may be listed as a $3.25 preferred or seven percent preferred stock.

Unless the preferred is adjustable or participating, the dividend rate stays the same but the yield fluctuates in relation to the preferred stock's market price. For example, a $2.10 preferred stock with a par value of $30 per share initially yields seven percent when sold at par. However, if the preferred stock price rises to $40 per share, the stock now only yields 5 1/4 percent ($2.10/$40). Conversely, if the stock price decreases to $25 per share, the yield will rise to 8.4 percent ($2.10/$25).

There are a number of key factors to take into consideration when deciding to purchase a preferred stock. First of all, take a good hard look at the underlying credit of the issuing company. Investigate how both the shares and debt issues are rated. What has been the company's long-term credit track record? Are there problems looming on the industry's or company's horizon that could impact the firm's ability to pay dividends as scheduled?

"Make sure the issue has protection in the case of a takeover," advises Prudential's Bice.

Be sure to examine the call provisions and call protection of the issue. Generally, most preferreds are noncallable for five years, protecting the investor for that length of time or the remaining period of time before the initial call date if market interest rates decline. Once the stock becomes callable and prevailing interest rates drop lower than the preferred dividend rate, the issuer is likely to call or retire the stock.

"Do not overweight your portfolio with straight preferreds. Many can be called and will be if interest rates go down to the detriment of the investor expecting a certain yield and income stream in future years. On the other hand, should rates rise capital losses are likely," warns Charles Roden, managing director in charge of the fixed income department of Josephthal Lyon & Ross Inc., in New York.

When investigating a preferred stock, make sure you analyze the company's ability to cover the preferred stock dividend payments. You can determine a firm's preferred dividend coverage by dividing net income after interest and taxes and before common stock dividends by the dollar amount of the preferred stock dividends.

This calculation exercise lets you know how many times current earnings or anticipated earnings cover the preferred dividend payout.

As mentioned earlier, the presence of additional features such as minimum working capital requirements and sinking fund requirements add to the particular issue's relative attractiveness in comparison to other preferreds and other investment alternatives.

Finally, compare preferred pricing and yield to other investments to make sure you don't overpay for an issue.

Table 7–1 provides a handy recap of the reasons investors find preferreds an enticing investment alternative.

Table 7–1
PREFERRED STOCK CHARACTERISTICS

Characteristic	Description
Senior Status	Preferreds carry a senior status over common stock with preferential treatment as to dividends and claim to ownership of corporate assets.

Credit Ratings	Preferred investors can choose from a wide range of credit quality from very conservative to aggressive high yields for more risky investments. See discussion on credit ratings later in this chapter.
Higher Yields	Preferreds typically offer higher yields over both common stock and straight bonds. Favored tax status and some limitations on voting rights, etc., contribute to higher yields.
Marketability and Liquidity	Preferreds are traded on major exchanges just like their common stock counterparts. While the liquidity of each particular preferred stock depends on the amount of float and investor interest, in general, ample liquidity exists for most preferreds. Low par values attract individual investors, providing depth to liquidity.
Smaller Funds Commitment	Because many preferred issues offer shares in $25 denominations, the cash outlay to build a diversified portfolio of preferred issues is usually less than that required for a portfolio of bonds.
Price Stability	Since preferreds possess the attributes of both common stock and fixed income securities, the preferred stock price movements are less pronounced then the volatility of the common stock.
Price Support	The fixed income feature of the preferred tends to support its stock market price because it will trade more like a straight bond, reacting to interest rates. Since the primary goal of preferred investing is to receive higher yields with less risk posture than that offered by common stock, the preferred stock price will be supported by its fixed income attribute (assuming the dividend paying ability of the company has not been impaired) while the common stock price may continue to drift lower at a faster rate.
Fixed Dividend Rate	Known income stream and yield since the dividend rate is known upfront. Aids investor in planning for required income streams to meet future financial commitments.

Perpetual Life	While bonds have a specified limited life, preferred stock life is unlimited, subject to call provisions. This means the investor can be assured of a fixed income stream. On the other side of the coin, if interest rates rise and the current yield of the preferred stock drops, investor interest may decrease and push the preferred stock price down.
Quarterly Income	Like common stocks and unlike bonds, preferred stocks pay their dividends quarterly. If you require a regular monthly income stream, you will need to construct a portfolio of preferreds with varying payment dates to achieve a monthly income stream.

Optional Characteristics

Cumulative Feature	Some preferreds carry a cumulative clause which allows them to carry forward any skipped or unpaid dividends until the company is once again financially able to resume dividend payments. All dividends in arrears on preferred stock must be paid before resumption of common stock dividends.
Participating Feature	Allows preferred stockholders to receive an additional dividend above and beyond the regular preferred dividend, in the event of improved company earnings performance. In other words, preferred shareholders participate in the good fortunes of the company.
Convertible Feature	Some preferreds are convertible into shares of common stock under specified conditions. This permits the preferred investor to more fully share in the upside potential of a rise in the market price of common stock as the company's financial performance improves.
Adjustable Rate Feature	The adjustable rate provision provides interest rate risk protection by adjusting the dividend rate based on changes in an interest rate composite.

Just as you would with any other investment options, you need to check on the risk attributable to purchasing a preferred security. This is relatively easy to accomplish. For example, Standard & Poor's maintains and monthly updates preferred stock ratings. Your broker can provide you with a copy of *Standard & Poor's Stock Guide*. Check your library for a copy or you can subscribe directly to the guide by calling 1-800-221-5277.

Preferred stock ratings changes are conveniently located near the front of the guide, indicating both the old rating and the new rating. This lets you know if the credit quality of the preferred issue is improving or eroding. On the same page, a listing of "New Insertions" into the guide and a table of "Listings Pending" tip you off to new preferred issues or issues gaining initial coverage in *Standard & Poor's Stock Guide*, typically a good sign for increased investor knowledge and liquidity.

Rating Preferred Stock—The S&P Rating System

The Standard & Poor's preferred stock rating system strives to assess the capacity and willingness of the issuer to pay preferred stock dividends and any applicable sinking fund obligations. It is important to note that since the preferred stock issue is subordinate to any company debt issue, the rating of the preferred stock normally is not higher than the bond rating for senior debt of the same issuer. Given the above, S & P derives the preferred stock rating from a combination of assessments of the likelihood of the preferred dividend payment; nature of, and provisions of, the issue; and the relative position of the particular issue in the event of bankruptcy, reorganization, or other arrangements affecting creditors' rights.

Table 7–2 lists definitions of the preferred stock rating symbols used by Standard & Poor's Corporation. It is extremely important to know and understand the symbols and the ramifications of the ratings and changes in ratings in order to properly assess your own investment risk posture and to properly construct or adjust your investment portfolio to remain within your acceptable risk parameters.

Table 7–2
PREFERRED STOCK RATING SYMBOLS AND DESCRIPTIONS

Preferred Stock Rating	Rating Description
"AAA"	Highest S&P rating indicating an extremely strong capacity for meeting its preferred stock dividend payment and other preferred obligations.
"AA"	Qualifying as a high quality fixed income security with a very strong capacity to pay preferred stock obligations but not as strong as the "AAA" rating.
"A"	Security backed by a sound capacity to pay the preferred stock obligations but more susceptible to the adverse effects of changes in circumstances and economic conditions.
"BBB"	Backed by adequate capacity to pay preferred stock obligations. However, adverse economic conditions or deteriorating circumstances more likely to lead to a weakened capacity to meet obligations.
"BB", "B", "CCC"	These preferred ratings indicate conditions predominately speculative in regard to the issuer's capability to meet preferred obligations. In other words, major risk exposures to adverse conditions and large uncertainties outweigh positive quality factors and protective characteristics of the issue. The degree of speculation rises as you move from the "BB" rating to the "CCC" rating.
"CC"	Indicates a preferred stock issue already in arrears on its dividends or sinking fund requirements but that is currently paying.
"C"	A nonpaying preferred stock issue.
"D"	A nonpaying preferred stock issue with its issuer in default on debt securities.

"NR"   No rating has been requested, insufficient
                         information exists on which to base a rating, or
                         Standard and Poor's Corporation does not rate
                         this specific type of obligation as a matter of
                         internal corporate policy.

In addition to these ratings, S&P uses a Plus (+) or Minus (–) symbol to represent even more intricate indications of a preferred stock quality in order to more accurately reflect its relative standing within the major rating categories illustrated above.

The body of the stock guide provides a wealth of valuable information on each preferred. Besides the preferred S&P rating, you can readily determine the preferred issue's name and dividend rate, ticker symbol, the call price of the preferred, the year in which the call price declines (located in the footnotes), other preferred provisions, the stock exchange on which the preferred trades, trading units, outstanding shares, par value, institutional ownership, current yield, and dividend payment date as well as company financial and operating statistics.

For example, a little sleuthing in the stock guide uncovers the following information on a preferred issue of San Francisco-based bank holding company, Bank America Corporation: the preferred stock is a 6.5 percent cumulative series G issue convertible into 1.09649 shares of Bank America common stock at a conversion rate of $45.60 per share.

It trades in units of 100 shares on the New York Stock Exchange under the ticker symbol Pr G, and has no par value. At the end of 1992, 15 institutions held over four million of the preferred shares. This preferred issue garnered a BBB+ rating from Standard & Poor's Corporation. It pays a quarterly dividend of $.81 1/4 per share for an annual dividend payout of $3.25 per share. At the end of 1992, it yielded 5.34 percent. There were five million preferred shares of this issue outstanding.

The issue's call price stands at $51.95 per share from May 31, 1995 and scales down to $50 per share in the year 2001.

Other information includes stock price trading ranges for various time frames, trading volume for most recent month, company book value, long-term debt, common and preferred stock capitalization, and earnings per share for recent years, and the latest quarter's earnings per share versus last year's similar results.

Another valuable source of information on preferred stocks is *The Value Line Investment Survey*. It can be found in most libraries. By referring to the "Capital Structure" section of Figure 7-1, Bank America Corporation, you can see that the financial institution also issued a number of other preferred stocks including a Series A $50 stated value, cumulative, adjustable rate (currently $3.35) preferred; a Series B, $100 stated value, cumulative, adjustable rate (currently $6.00) preferred; and a Series F, $25 cumulative preferred redeemable at par after April 15, 1996.

Just as you keep tabs on changing S&P ratings on your preferreds or ones you are considering purchasing, keep a close pulse on the institution ownership information mentioned earlier. It can indicate changing sentiments about the prospects of the underlying company and also potential pressure (either upward or downward) on the preferred's stock price.

Not only do you have to watch the firm's financial and operating progress, as a preferred investor you also have to closely monitor the interest rate environment. Since the preferred issue tends to trade like a straight bond due to its fixed dividend, changes in interest rates will directly impact the preferred issue's stock price.

THE MUTUAL FUND ROUTE

If you want to pass along the overall management of preferred stock picking to professional managers you might consider a specialized mutual fund such as The Vanguard Preferred Stock Fund.

This preferred stock mutual fund earned a total return of 34.5 percent for the two fiscal years ended October 31, 1992. Over the long-term horizon, for the 15-year period ended October 31, 1992; Vanguard Preferred Stock Fund earned a cumulative return of 334 percent and an average annual total return of 10.3 percent compared to 287 percent and 9.4 percent, respectively, for the average fixed income mutual fund.

For the six months ended April 30, 1993, Vanguard Preferred Stock Fund earned a total return of 7.7 percent compared with 5.7 percent for the Merrill Lynch Perpetual Preferred Index, a broad measure of the preferred stock market comprising more than 60 preferred issues having a total market value in excess of $3 billion. During this six-month time frame, the preferred fund also outperformed the 6.3 percent return achieved by the average fixed income mutual fund.

Vanguard points out that their higher returns by investing in preferreds over traditional fixed income instruments comes with an element of higher risk from two fronts. In comparison to bonds, preferreds possess a higher degree of credit risk since preferreds assume a junior status to debt instruments. Likewise, preferred investors face higher market risk exposure since their longer maturities (sometimes perpetual) create more price volatility in relation to bonds possessing shorter maturities.

Each individual investor must measure and evaluate for him or herself the degree of additional risk he or she desires to take on to achieve higher returns. For those willing to assume incremental risks, earning higher returns by investing in preferred stocks remains a viable option.

The Vanguard Preferred Stock Fund invests in preferreds with quality ratings as follows: "AAA" (four percent), "AA" (18 percent), "A" (41 percent), and "BBB" (37 percent), all investment grade securities. Providing stabilization to the fund's net asset value, management invests some six percent in sinking fund preferreds. Also providing a degree of security, about 57 percent of fund assets are concentrated in approximately 62 electric and gas utility industry preferred issues. These issuers' earnings provide more than two times coverage of their preferred dividend obligations.

Utility preferred holdings as of April 30, 1993, were Alabama Power Company 7.6 percent (A rating), Baltimore Gas & Electric 7.78 percent (A rating), Detroit Edison Company 7.75 percent

(BBB rating), Iowa Illinois Gas & Electric Company 7.50 percent (AA rating), P.S.I. Energy, Inc., 7.44 percent (BBB rating), San Diego Gas & Electric Company $7.05 and $7.20 (both A ratings), and Wisconsin Electric Power Company 6.75 percent (AA+ rating).

Banking, finance, industrial, insurance, and telephone preferreds in the Vanguard stable include Key Corp 10 percent (BBB rating), Norwest Corporation 10.24 percent (A rating), Republic New York Corporation 7.75 percent (A+ rating), Beneficial Corporation $4.30 (A rating), Aluminum Company of America $3.75 (A+ rating), E.I. duPont de Nemours & Company $4.50 (AA rating), Old Republic International Corporation 8.75 percent (A+ rating), and GTE North, Inc., $7.60 (AA rating).

Another way to play the preferred market, at least partially, lies in investing in utility mutual funds which have a proportion of their holdings in utility preferred issues.

Investors can also take a global approach to preferred investing. Due to a tax agreement between the United States and the United Kingdom, both the issuing company and individual investors can receive a tax credit for preferred tax issues. For example, under the tax agreement, both Barclay's Bank and the Royal Bank of Scotland have issued preferred stock in the United States.

Another relatively new twist on the preferred scene is the corporate note convertible into a preferred security. This is issued as a corporate note and the holder can convert the note into a preferred security under specified conditions.

For example, in 1993 Bankers Trust New York Corporation issued a 7 5/8 percent convertible capital security (note) to mature on June 1, 2033. The interest rate can be reset by the company at any time upon not more than 90 or less than 60 days notice to the security holders. The holders then have the option of converting their capital securities into Depositary Shares, each representing a one-tenth interest in a share of the corporation's Series O, 7 5/8 percent cumulative preferred stock.

Preferred securities are drawing a lot of attention from both corporations and individual investors. Preferred underwritings have increased dramatically in the past few years. According to

Security Data Corporation in Newark, New Jersey, in 1990, companies floated 111 issues worth $10.4 billion. That grew to 231 issues worth $20.9 billion in 1992. The torrid pace has not let up. For the first six months in 1993, corporations floated 133 issues worth $11.4 billion.

Whichever way you decide to participate in the preferred market, you need to assess investment grades and yield differentials with alternative investments. In addition, don't forget those call provisions which could affect your investment performance and risk posture.

Check into the preferred options available to you. You could find yourself receiving preferential treatment in terms of higher yield and overall returns.

8

selling
short

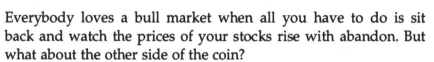

Everybody loves a bull market when all you have to do is sit back and watch the prices of your stocks rise with abandon. But what about the other side of the coin?

Too many investors sit idly by during markets with a bearish trend, waiting for the economy and the stock market to change direction and head upward once more. Unfortunately, most investors fail to realize that just as much money, if not substantially more, can be made on the downside of a market move as on its upside.

Think of it like this. Have you ever seen any football team that fields just an offense? Of course not, because the defense plays an integral part of the coach's overall winning strategy. In fact, it's often the defense that sets up the winning score in the toughest games.

When stock prices start heading south, it's time to seriously consider whether or not to sell stocks that you don't own. You read the above sentence correctly. The art and science of short selling involves selling stocks you don't own by first borrowing them from your broker, who in turn borrows them from a third party.

Despite belief to the contrary, the basic short selling strategy is simple. You sell a borrowed stock now at a high price with the anticipation that you can purchase it back later at a low enough price to cover your interest and commission expenses and have a tidy profit left over.

Short selling strategy rests on your conviction, after proper analysis, that stock prices in general or for a specific firm will drop in the weeks and months ahead.

Human nature being what it is, we love to back a winner. Some folks even feel that short selling is tantamount to being un-American, betting against the good fortunes of U.S. companies. The plain truth is that the companies' fortunes won't change one iota whether you purchase their stock or not. Since you typically acquire or sell stock in the secondary markets on major stock exchanges or over-the-counter, your short selling does not directly impact the firm's financial position.

It could be argued that short sellers drive stock prices down by exerting downward pressure. This is certainly true; however, the real reason behind the downward price pressure ultimately stems from the firm's future revenue and earnings prospects. The short seller actually makes the market more efficient by recognizing and acting on the firm's deteriorating condition and prospects.

The financial facts of life dictate that you must keep your investment capital at work during all times of the investment cycle to maximize your return. Get your defense on the field during down markets and take advantage of management fumbles with well-thought out and executed short selling.

Don't let your investments stagnate, or even worse, suffer losses during down markets. Strategic short selling profits can help offset those inevitable losses incurred during bear markets.

A popular analogy for explaining short selling goes like this. Assume you believe the price of cows is way too high. You want to capitalize on the high price of cows by selling one now and buying one back later at a lower price. Unfortunately, you do not own any cows. However, your neighbor owns one cow. You make an agreement to borrow your neighbor's cow for replacement at a later date with a cow of equal quality. You take it to the cow market and sell it for $1,000, the current going rate for cows. Several months later, the price of cows has dropped to $500, as you wisely anticipated. You now purchase a cow at that price, return the cow to your neighbor and pocket the $500 difference or profit less any transaction and borrowing costs. You made money on the deal; the neighbor is happy because he or she made interest on the borrowed cow and has an equal cow back. That's how short selling works.

During bull markets, euphoria takes over and stock prices tend to get bid up over their underlying values. Even in the midst of the recent prolonged recession or economic stagnation, stock market prices continued to hit new highs, seemingly defying reality.

It would appear that only a complete fool would be selling stocks in the face of a continuing bull market. But don't kid yourself. There have been ample opportunities for short selling profits during the recent market rise in light of volatile price swings in the market overall, in market segments, and in particular stocks.

For instance, despite a rise in the Dow Jones Industrial Average from the 3200 level at the beginning of 1993, to over 3600 by mid-August, 1993, the market experienced a number of sharp pullbacks of more than 100 points each over varying periods of time.

Likewise, healthcare industry stocks were battered during the first half of 1993, due to uncertainties associated with pending health care reform legislation. The gaming industry represents another example of how stocks get overpriced, ready for a tumble, and short selling profits for the astute investor.

The explosion in states allowing gaming operations created a euphoria that sent the stock prices of gaming industry companies soaring. In fact, gaming stocks outperformed every other industry group tracked by *Investor's Business Daily* from the beginning of

October 1992 through the first half of 1993. The gaming index of 44 stocks surged some 63 percent over that time frame.

Market rationale went out the window when newly issued gaming stocks with no prior track record, shaky financials, and poor earnings prospects or even losses shot up to week after week of new highs. To be sure, quality gaming firms such as International Game Technology with secure market share, strong domestic, and overseas franchises, and proven technology should continue to hit pay dirt in their venues and earnings columns; however, the current explosion in gaming firm stock prices clearly represents the impressive fundamentals of the quality firms pulling along the mediocre firms.

In other words, and you heard it here first, expect a dramatic shakeout in the gaming industry firms and their stock prices. Studying the industry, market niches and potential, company and management strengths and weaknesses, and company financial capabilities can help you sort out the winners from the losers, those which could be shorted for exceptional investment gains.

As noted above, short selling opportunities come about for a variety of reasons and scenarios. The overall market could have rushed ahead to high levels which can not be sustained by economic reality, thus, may be poised for a deep pullback. Investors may have overreacted to good news about an individual company or industry and the stock prices will have to consolidate their gains by back-tracking a bit. Or a company may be headed for tough economic times ahead and the market has failed to fully take this into account in current stock price levels, setting up the stock prices for a fall in the future.

Some short selling opportunities are isolated instances such as the overbuying of gaming stocks in late 1992 and 1993. Other short selling situations arise due to regular or periodic economic cycles. For example, it's well known that certain industries and firms follow cyclical patterns.

The revenue and profit levels of paper companies, steel firms, and automobile manufacturers are geared to changes in the economy to varying degrees and timing factors. It would be foolish to purchase shares in General Motors Corporation or USX Corporation in the face of an economic slow down and antici-pated market peak. On the other hand, a short position in those stocks at that time could deliver extraordinary investment gains while other investors watch their stock prices tumble and losses mount.

To participate in the world of short selling, it is important to know and understand the game rules. First of all, in order to sell short you need to establish a margin account with your broker. See Chapter Four, Managing Margin. You will need to put up either cash or marginable securities as collateral.

With the current 50 percent margin rules in affect, you can short $2 worth of stock for every $1 worth of collateral residing in your margin account. It's wise to keep a collateral safety cushion to prevent unwanted margin calls from forcing you out of a stock or short position.

Don't look for dividends to help increase your short position investment return. Any dividends accruing to the stock belong to the owner of the stock, the person from whom the shorted stock was borrowed.

A short sale must always be made at either a price higher than the last sale or at the same price of the last sale, if the last preceding change in the security's price was upward. In no case can a short sale take place at a price lower than the previous sale. This is called the "short sale," "uptick," or "plus tick" rule.

The purpose of the "uptick" rule is to prevent short selling from driving the price of a particular security down further in a declining market and potentially causing a panic situation and downward price spiral. This "uptick" rule can also result in your broker taking longer to complete your short trade.

All stocks cannot be sold short. Generally speaking, stocks selling for under $5 a share cannot be sold short. In addition, you cannot short stocks in odd lots, you must short stocks in round lots (typically 100 shares).

Perhaps the biggest deterrent preventing most individual in-vestors from short selling, after overcoming the psychological factor of selling what you don't own, stems from the possibility of unlimited loss.

When you establish a long position in a stock at a price of $15 per share, your maximum exposure is $15 per share, the amount you have committed to invest. If the company goes bankrupt and you don't receive any proceeds from the liquidation, your loss is limited to the $15 per share.

Taking a short position, however, means you assume a potentially unlimited loss position. If you short the stock at $15 per share, it could rise to $100 per share or more. Of course, prudence demands that you close out your short position and cut your losses long before the stock reaches the $100 per share level.

Another way to reduce the risk of unlimited loss on short sales is to buy a call option on the stock you decide to short sell. If the stock price rises and your short position loses value, your call option increases in value. Once the stock price is above the exercise price of the option, the call will offset any losses from your short position on a point-per-point basis. See Chapter Six, Options.

If the stock does decline as you anticipate, your short position makes money and the call option, at the very worst, expires worthless. The minimal premium you paid for the call served as a risk reduction or insurance program against the possibility of the stock price rising.

Depending on the length of your short position, you may have to purchase several call options, one replacing another as it expires.

Another tactic to reduce your risk of short selling involves having a long position in the stock you short. This "short against the box" strategy assures a no net change in profit or loss no matter which direction the stock price moves. This is an excellent way to protect existing gains from your long position in the stock or protect short selling profits from a rise in the stock's price.

Some investors use "short against the box," tactics for tax planning purposes. It works like this. When you sell your securities outright, you incur a tax liability on the gain or loss right away and reportable in the current tax year.

By selling "short against the box," you gain the advantage of using the cash generated from the sale immediately but defer the gain or loss realized on the transaction until you cover the short position. If you wait until the next tax year to cover your short position, you have delayed your tax liability one year without sacrificing use of the money in the meantime. In fact, since there are no restrictions on how long a short position can be left open, you can delay your tax liability almost indefinitely.

"Short Against the Box" Case Study

To illustrate the "short against the box" principle, assume you purchased the stock of ABC Company for $15 per share several years ago. The firm's revenues and earnings have continued on an impressive uptrend and its stock price has followed suit, moving up nicely to its current level of $30 per share.

While you still have faith in corporate management to keep the record revenues and earnings strings intact, the overall economy and level of stock market prices have you worried. You don't want to sell your stock and forgo further price increases; yet, you don't like the added risk inherent in the above uncertainties.

By going "short against the box," selling the stock short while maintaining your long position, you protect the gain, $15 per share less commissions, you have already earned to date.

If the market and ABC's stock stagnates at the same level, you have protected your gain and can postpone your tax liability until you cover your short position. If the stock price declines, you have also protected your gain. If the stock price rises, you won't be able to participate in any further gains because the short and long positions cancel each other out.

Once you have determined the new trend, you can shed either the long or short position and once again participate in the stock's price moves.

ANOTHER RISK REDUCTION STRATEGY

Another way to reduce your risk in short selling is to place a "buy-stop" order after your short position has been established. This triggers a purchase of the stock, closing out your short position, when the stock hits a certain price. You have to be careful where you set "buy-stop" orders so you don't get stopped out too soon and lose the opportunity to earn short selling profits when the stock price heads down again. Factor in the market's volatility and the volatility of the individual stock when setting your stop limits.

Keep a good pulse on the fortunes and/or misfortunes of the companies you plan on shorting. Know how anticipated changes in the economic, political, legal and social environment can impact their future performance and the level of their stock prices.

Stock market trends represent an important barometer for the short seller. The old stock market adage, "the trend is your friend," goes double for this strategy.

Stay away from stocks continuing to make new highs. Don't let the expectation that they must tumble soon cloud your investment analysis. Momentum is a powerful stock market force and must be reckoned with. It's like trying to stop a freight train by putting a marshmallow on the track. Wait for a consolidation and pullback for indications of a slow-down, then search for confirmation of a sustainable price reversal.

Closely related to the high price scenario, the high price/earnings (P/E) ratio method of ferreting out companies whose stocks should be sold short, often fails to produce profitable results. Again, it's hard to fight momentum. P/E ratios may help locate potential stocks which could be sold short in the future but you need more evidence before you place the stock on the final short selling list.

Followers of technical analysis charting techniques point to the head-and-shoulders figure as confirmation of unique short selling opportunities. For an in-depth discussion of head-and-shoulders and other charting techniques see Chapter Two, Technical Predictors, of my investment book, *Divining The Dow* (Probus, 1993), a Fortune Book Club selection.

Others point to stocks which have broken through their consolidation or support levels as likely short selling candidates.

Steer clear of stocks with little float. A lack of liquidity can translate into large price rises on small volume, causing large losses and a possible margin call. Thinly traded stocks could also be hard to replace at a favorable price if the "lendor" requests them back from your broker.

Be wary of selling short a weak performer in a strong group. The upward movement of the group could override the fundamentals of the one weak company in the industry. This does not mean to avoid short selling in the group altogether, but you better be aware of the potential consequences. As mentioned earlier, a number of companies in the gaming industry appear to be way over-valued, ripe for short selling at the opportune moment.

Don't forget to use "buy-stop" orders and consider purchasing call options and selling "short against the box" when appropriate to reduce the amount of risk you are willing to assume. Short selling pundits recommend establishing "buy-stops" between 10 percent to 25 percent above the price at which you shorted the stock.

Substantial short interest in a stock may indicate you have already missed the bandwagon. If the stock starts to advance, a large short interest position could fuel a major advance in the firm's stock price as short sellers scramble to cover their outstanding short positions.

Don't jump into short selling whole hog. It takes a much different mental perspective than traditional stock market investing. Learn to walk before you run. Even after you become savvy in the ways of short selling, confine the strategy to a relatively small proportion of your overall diversified investment strategy. See Chapter One, Diversification Techniques.

While high P/E stocks could indicate future short selling candidates, don't forget to investigate low P/E stocks. Firms with P/Es lower than their industry or other group counterparts tend to retreat faster during an economic downturn and trail during an upturn. Many low P/E stocks have earned their lower ratios with sub-standard performance and bleak future prospects.

Insider trading activity can signal opportunities for short selling. Corporate officers typically don't like to liquidate their holdings in company stock and insider selling could be a tipoff to a pending downturn in corporate earnings and stock prices.

You have to be very careful when interpreting insider sales. Other factors could come into the picture causing insiders to sell their company stock holdings. For instance, cash required to finance college expenses or a down payment needed on a new house could result in insiders shedding company shares without any negative reflection on the company's future prospects. It's also important to look at the size and proportion of the holdings being liquidated. Is it a relatively substantial stake in the company or a good percentage of the insider's company stock? The number of insiders selling also adds importance to the insider selling occurring. A single sale by one corporate insider may have no bearing whatsoever on the analysis of the company's prospects, but a number of sales by different corporate insiders bears more investigation.

Proponents of the insider theory track the insider sales ratio, computed as insider sales divided by insider purchases. As a guide, if the 10-week moving average calculates to less than 1.5, its a positive sign indicating insiders are selling company shares at a slow pace. If the ratio rises above 3.0, short sellers take note because insiders have become heavy sellers, possibly indicating an overvalued situation.

For those interested in tracking insider trading more closely, Standard & Poor's *The Outlook* periodically reports on inside trades and there are a number of publications that specialize in information on inside trades such as *The Insiders* from The Institute for Econometric Research, 3417 North Federal Highway, Fort Lauderdale, Florida 33306, 800-442-9000, $100 annual subscription rate, published twice a month and *Vickers Weekly Insider* published by Vickers Stock Corporation, 226 New York Avenue, Huntington, New York 11743, 516-423-7710. An annual subscription costs $152.

Some short selling advocates suggest that stocks which have far outperformed market indices over the past 12 months are good short selling candidates. Remember, its wise to wait for confirmation signs of a sustained price reversal in progress.

Others recommend a close reading of the company's income statement, balance sheet, and source and use of funds statement to uncover potential problems that could negatively impact operations and profits in the months and years ahead. Over-leveraged situations, cash shortages and negative cash flow, restrictive credit arrangements, declining gross margins, rising expense ratios, etc., all point to problem areas that company management must recognize and successfully deal with in order to keep earnings rising and the firm's stock price up.

If you enter the short selling arena, it's important to keep appraised of the short interest (the amount of shares shorted) on each stock you are tracking and the trend in that short interest. In other words, is it increasing or decreasing and by how much. These numbers are reported monthly in the financial press such as *Barron's*, *Investor's Business Daily*, and *The Wall Street Journal*. These listings reflect the number of outstanding shares borrowed compared with the previous month for overall short interest positions of 10,000 shares or more. An increasing open interest indicates more investors believe the stock price will decline and vice versa.

There's another side to this coin that must be considered. The larger the short position, the greater the demand for shares (to replace borrowed ones) which can push the stock price higher. That leads us to the Short Interest Indicator which measures the ratio of short interest for a specific month to average daily market volume for a specific stock.

Followers of the short interest indicator believe that a large short position is bullish for the stock's future price performance because of the pent-up demand for that stock. In addition, a market swing upward could create a "short squeeze" situation, forcing short sellers to cover their open positions, thus, driving the stock price up even higher and creating even more "short squeeze" repurchases and still higher stock prices.

Short interest advocates also believe a surge in short positions often takes place near market bottoms, signalling caution to would-be short sellers.

To calculate the short interest ratio for a specific stock, divide monthly short interest figure by the average daily volume of the stock. For example, if ABC Company's short interest for a given month totaled 150,000 shares and the average daily volume stood at 30,000 shares, then ABC's short interest ratio would calculate out to 5.0. In other words, the short position represents five full days of trading in ABC shares.

Shortex, a publication specializing in short selling, sells for $279 for an annual subscription or $159 for a six month trial. It can be ordered from Technomart R.G.A.-Investment Advisors, 6669 Security Boulevard, Suite 103, Baltimore, Maryland 21207-4014 or call 800-877-6555 for information.

Short Selling Cases

Back in mid-1990, a number of investment specialists were advocating short selling Sara Lee (NYSE: SLE). In fact, short interest in Sara Lee shares soared to nearly four million shares. With an average daily volume around 586,000 shares, the short interest amounted to nearly seven days worth of trading.

By mid-1990, the diversified bakery and consumer products firm's stock price had drifted 20 percent lower to $26 3/4 per share despite 13 years of record earnings. The shorts clearly anticipated that Sara Lee was due for a continued fall in stock price.

Were they right? Yes, but only for a short time. The shorts did accurately anticipate a further Sara Lee stock price decline but only to the $24 1/8 per share level reached in July/August 1990 before the company's stock rebounded strongly. The shorts who were nimble enough to have exited their short positions before Fall officially began probably made some short selling profits.

The others most likely took a beating as the price of Sara Lee stock soared to a high of $58 per share in late 1991, with only a brief consolidation period in mid-1991. See Figure 8–1, Sara Lee Corporation. To be sure, many short sellers lost their shirts, getting "short squeezed" out of their short positions as Sara Lee's stock price rose dramatically on two more years of record profits in both 1991 and 1992.

The moral is simple. Short selling like purchasing long positions can work both ways. You need to properly investigate before you buy or short sell any stock. Looking back, it's easy to evaluate that the Sara Lee short sellers let a "short selling frenzy" overrule the company's solid fundamentals and stellar track record.

The short sellers focused on temporary growth slowdowns and potential problems in one market segment (t-shirts, accounting for only two percent of company revenues) to their own detriment. Instead, they should have been looking at the big picture.

Sara Lee had a well-established international marketing system firmly in place to expand international revenues and earnings. The company put into motion programs to increase efficiency and reduce costs which paid off big in higher margins. It's important to note that these advances were accomplished in a recessionary economy both domestically and in the international market.

Figure 8–1
SARA LEE CORPORATION

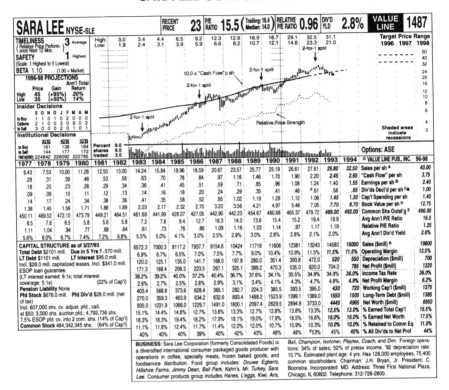

Source: Reprinted by permission. Copyright 1993, Value Line Publishing, Inc. All rights reserved.

Sara Lee short sellers would have been well advised to heed "the trend is your friend" adage in terms of Sara Lee's ability to deliver on revenue and earnings gains.

INTERNATIONAL GAME TECHNOLOGY

Another stock being touted as a short sale candidate in mid-1990 was gaming giant International Game Technology. Again, the short sellers missed the jackpot. They choose to short a leading company in an explosive industry.

Needless to say, International Game Technology lead the pack of gaming firms which solidly outpaced all other industry groups tracked by *Investor's Business Daily.* Instead of declining, International Game Technology 's stock price surged like a rocket on July 4th, splitting a number of times before hitting a high of $39 3/4 per share in 1993. See Figure 8–2, International Game Technology.

Figure 8–2
INTERNATIONAL GAME TECHNOLOGY

INT'L GAME TECHNOL. NYSE-IGT	RECENT PRICE **38**	P/E RATIO **44.7** (Trailing: 53.5 Median: 17.0)	RELATIVE P/E RATIO **2.71**	DIV'D YLD **0.6%**	VALUE LINE **1781**

	1977	1978	1979	1980	1981	1982	1983	1984	1985	1986	1987	1988	1989	1990	1991	1992	1993	1994	© VALUE LINE PUB., INC.	96-98
	--	--	--	.17	.36	.50	.50	.47	.57	.44	.40	1.02	.86	1.29	1.86	2.11	3.42	3.85	4.15	Sales per sh A	6.90
	--	--	--	.03	.09	.14	.09	.10	.12	.05	.01	.09	.12	.17	.26	.38	.72	.90	1.40	"Cash Flow" per sh	2.25
	--	--	.01	.07	.12	.06	.07	.09	.01	d.06	.01	.08	.11	.17	.26	.52	.75	1.15	Earnings per sh B	2.00
	--	--	--	--	--	--	--	--	--	--	--	--	--	--	--	.06	.30	Div'ds Decl'd per sh C	.48
	--	--	.04	.06	.07	.09	.07	.07	.06	.08	.12	.08	.14	.13	.20	.29	.25	.25	Cap'l Spending per sh	.40
	--	--	.02	.11	.27	.34	.41	.50	.51	.46	.38	.58	.70	.82	1.10	1.83	2.75	4.05	Book Value per sh	7.15
	--	--	107.44	109.18	123.78	125.25	126.74	128.52	129.13	129.35	81.96	114.94	117.47	112.84	112.51	116.69	124.00	135.00	Common Shs Outst'g D	130.35
	--	--	--	--	7.3	12.9	11.1	11.1	65.9	--	93.4	11.3	14.4	11.3	15.2	26.1	Bold figures are	Avg Ann'l P/E Ratio	20.0
	--	--	--	--	.89	1.42	.94	1.03	5.35	--	6.24	.94	1.09	.84	.97	1.58	Value Line estimates	Relative P/E Ratio	1.55
	--	--	--	--	--	--	--	--	--	--	--	--	--	--	--	--		Avg Ann'l Div'd Yield	1.2%

CAPITAL STRUCTURE as of 3/31/93
Total Debt $97.3 mill.   Due in 5 Yrs $7.0 mill.
LT Debt $95.7 mill.   LT Interest $8.2 mill.
Incl. $76.6 mill., 8.5% subord. notes conv. to common at $7.87/sh., redeemable 6/94.
Excl. $86.7 mill. in liabilities to Progressive Jackpot Systems winners, offset by $68.3 mill. investments. Incl. $1.9 mill. capitalized leases.
(LT interest earned 8.9x; total interest coverage: 8.7x)   (24% of Cap'l)
Leases, Uncapitalized Annual rentals $2.4 mill.
Pension Liability None
Pfd Stock None
Common Stock 122,422,223 shs.   (76% of Cap'l)

60.0	73.3	56.6	52.1	83.5	98.7	151.2	210.3	237.4	399.4	480	560	Sales ($mill) A	900
40.3%	35.8%	17.4%	6.7%	18.3%	21.0%	18.2%	18.8%	23.8%	31.1%	32.0%	33.0%	Operating Margin	35.0%
4.2	4.3	4.4	8.9	6.7	5.5	6.6	9.4	12.0	19.0	19.0	21.0	Depreciation ($mill)	35.0
8.7	11.2	1.5	d7.1	.8	7.7	13.2	20.0	30.2	64.8	95.0	165	Net Profit ($mill)	260
45.3%	41.9%	20.5%	--	49.1%	37.2%	37.7%	37.4%	38.1%	39.5%	38.0%	36.0%	Income Tax Rate	36.0%
14.4%	15.2%	2.6%	NMF	1.0%	7.8%	8.7%	9.5%	12.7%	16.2%	19.8%	29.5%	Net Profit Margin	28.9%
24.7	32.2	32.7	23.5	31.8	48.1	68.3	80.5	184.1	257.1	145	170	Working Cap'l ($mill)	270
2.5	2.5	2.3	2.9	27.8	18.0	23.9	27.6	113.3	114.0	100	20.0	Long-Term Debt ($mill)E	29.0
52.4	64.5	66.1	60.0	30.7	67.1	82.0	92.7	123.8	214.1	340	545	Net Worth ($mill)	930
16.2%	16.8%	2.9%	NMF	4.8%	11.7%	14.6%	18.4%	14.7%	21.8%	22.5%	29.5%	% Earned Total Cap'l	27.0%
16.5%	17.3%	2.2%	NMF	2.6%	11.5%	16.1%	21.6%	24.4%	30.3%	28.0%	30.5%	% Earned Net Worth	28.0%
16.5%	17.3%	2.2%	NMF	2.6%	11.5%	16.1%	21.6%	24.4%	30.3%	26.0%	23.0%	% Retained to Comm Eq	21.0%
--	--	--	--	--	--	--	--	--	--	8%	24%	% All Div'ds to Net Prof	24%

BUSINESS: International Game Technology is the leading maker of casino gambling machines. Operates multi-site progressive slot systems (*Megabucks* et. al.) in Nevada and Atlantic City. Factory is in Reno. IGT-Australia subsid. makes and sells slot machines there. CMS-International (88%-owned) operates three casinos in Nevada and one on Antigua, in the Caribbean. Electronic Data Technologies (45%-owned) makes player tracking systems and operates Nevada gaming route. Sold interest in Syntech Int'l (4/88). 1992 depr. rate: 21%. Est'd plant age: 7 yrs. Has 1,400 shrhldrs., 2,150 empls. Insiders control 7% of stock. Chairman & C.E.O.: Charles N. Mathewson. Pres.: John J. Russell. Inc.: Nevada. Address: 520 South Rock Blvd., Reno, NV 89502. Tel.: 702-323-5060.

Suffice it to say that International Game Technology was the worst stock during that time frame to short.

The main point of the two above examples, is to do your own thorough investigation of the company and industry prospects. Don't rely on rumors or articles recommending short selling. Check out the facts for yourself before short selling.

Lest you think all short sales end in tragedy, take a look at the following short selling case study.

Oracle Systems Corporation

Oracle Systems Corporation (NASDAQ: ORCL) posted record earnings of 86 cents per share for fiscal year 1990 ended May 31, 1990. That amounted to a nearly 50 percent improvement over the prior fiscal year's results.

Oracle's stock price had risen dramatically from just a tad under $4 per share in late 1987 to over $28 per share, adjusted for several stock splits, in the first quarter of calendar year 1990.

Then Oracle ran into a buzzsaw. Revenue growth slowed dramatically in fiscal 1991 ended May 31, 1991, and coupled with high facility and personnel levels caused the world's largest manufacturer of database management systems to suffer a loss of nine cents per share.

This time the short sellers were right on target. Oracle's stock price crashed like a zapped mainframe, sending its per share price sinking below $5 per share before the end of calendar year 1990.

Management went to work to turn the company around and investors who followed the company closely could have turned their short selling gains into profits by going long on Oracle System's stock after it bottomed out just below $5 a share and rebounded to hit a high of $16 5/8 per share in 1991, $28 5/8 per share in 1992, and $53 3/4 per share by mid-1993 in 1993.

Figure 8–3
ORACLE SYSTEMS CORPORATION

ORACLE OTC-ORCL	RECENT PRICE **53**	P/E RATIO **41.7** (Trailing: 49.5 Median: NMF)	RELATIVE P/E RATIO **2.51**	DIV'D YLD **Nil**	VALUE LINE **2127**

TIMELINESS **1** Highest (Relative Price Perform-ance Next 12 Mos.)										
SAFETY **4** Below Average (Scale: 1 Highest to 5 Lowest)										
BETA 1.50 (1.00 = Market)										

| | High: | 3.6 | 9.5 | 11.1 | 26.0 | 28.4 | 16.6 | 28.6 | 56.9 |
| | Low: | 1.6 | 2.5 | 5.7 | 9.4 | 4.9 | 5.5 | 12.0 | 26.6 |

1996-98 PROJECTIONS

	Price	Gain	Ann'l Total Return
High	90	(+70%)	14%
Low	60	(+15%)	3%

Insider Decisions

	O	N	D	J	F	M	A	M	J
to Buy	0	0	0	0	0	0	0	0	0
Options	0	2	2	0	2	0	0	1	3
to Sell	0	7	4	0	2	0	0	3	5

Institutional Decisions

	4Q92	1Q93	2Q93
to Buy	89	107	99
to Sell	67	89	98
Hld's(000)	73217	81855	85036

Percent 30.0 / shares 20.0 / traded 10.0

Target Price Range 1996 1997 1998

2-for-1 split

16.0 x "Cash Flow" p sh

Relative Price Strength

Shaded areas indicate recessions

Options: CBOE

	1977	1978	1979	1980	1981	1982	1983	1984	1985	1986	1987	1988	1989	1990	1991	1992	1993	1994	© VALUE LINE PUB., INC.	96-98
	..	..	..	..	..	.03	.05	.13	.27	.53	1.14	2.35	4.60	7.40	7.54	8.42	10.57	13.85	Sales per sh^A	26.45
	..	..	..	..	..	..	..	.03	.07	.18	.47	.83	1.23	.43	.91	1.66	2.15	"Cash Flow" per sh	4.30
	..	..	..	..	..	.00	.01	.01	.02	.05	.13	.33	.61	.86	d.09	.43	1.07	1.50	Earnings per sh^B	3.40
	..	..	..	..	..	..	..	..	..	..	..	..	..	..	..	..	..	Nil	Div'ds Decl'd per sh	Nil
	..	..	..	..	..	..	..	.04	.11	.14	.26	.54	.68	.45	.33	.29	.55	Cap'l Spending per sh	.70
	..	..	..	..	.01	.01	.03	.08	.27	.72	1.12	1.82	2.96	2.53	3.11	3.71	5.05	Book Value per sh	12.95
	..	..	..	..	89.51	94.47	98.72	86.82	105.51	115.16	120.23	126.93	131.14	136.30	139.90	142.23	141.00	Common Shs Outst'g^C	140.00
	..	..	..	..	..	..	..	..	54.5	27.7	21.1	17.2	23.6	..	32.2	23.9		Avg Ann'l P/E Ratio	22.0
	..	..	..	..	..	..	..	..	3.70	1.85	1.75	1.30	1.75	..	1.95	1.43		Relative P/E Ratio	1.70
	..	..	..	..	..	..	..	..	..	..	..	..	..	..	..	..		Avg Ann'l Div'd Yield	Nil

CAPITAL STRUCTURE as of 5/31/93

Total Debt $97.1 mill. Due in 5 Yrs $16.9 mill.

LT Debt $86.4 mill. LT Interest $4.5 mill.
Incl. $15.4 mill.capitalized leases.
(Total interest coverage: 28.0x)
(14% of Cap'l)

Leases, Uncapitalized Annual rentals $72.1 mill.
Pension Liability None

Pfd Stock None

Common Stock 143,877,749 (86% of Cap'l)
as of 6/30/93

	1983	1984	1985	1986	1987	1988	1989	1990	1991	1992	1993	1994		96-98
	5.0	12.7	23.2	55.4	131.3	282.1	583.7	970.8	1027.9	1178.5	1502.8	1950	Sales ($mill)^A	3700
	..	15.9%	23.3%	25.7%	27.3%	25.0%	24.1%	8.6%	15.2%	21.3%	22.0%	Operating Margin	23.5%
	..	..	.9	2.0	5.3	13.0	23.2	44.1	70.7	65.8	79.2	85.0	Depreciation ($mill)	115
	.7	1.4	1.6	5.9	15.6	42.9	81.8	117.4	d12.4	61.5	156.4	220	Net Profit ($mill)	490
	..	..	38.5%	42.9%	44.1%	34.0%	31.9%	32.0%	32.0%	36.0%	35.4%	35.0%	Income Tax Rate	35.0%
	13.1%	10.9%	6.9%	10.6%	11.9%	15.2%	14.0%	12.1%	NMF	5.2%	10.4%	11.3%	Net Profit Margin	13.2%
	..	..	3.6	19.2	60.7	89.6	158.6	285.7	106.8	234.7	291.0	345	Working Cap'l ($mill)	1105
	.1	.2	1.4	5.6	9.0	5.4	33.5	89.1	18.0	95.9	86.4	85.0	Long-Term Debt ($mill)	85.0
	1.2	2.7	7.3	28.7	82.7	134.6	230.6	387.6	344.7	435.0	528.0	710	Net Worth ($mill)	1815
	48.2%	47.8%	19.0%	17.9%	17.4%	30.9%	31.4%	25.5%	NMF	12.2%	25.8%	28.0%	% Earned Total Cap'l	26.0%
	53.7%	51.7%	21.9%	20.6%	18.9%	31.9%	35.5%	30.3%	NMF	14.1%	29.6%	31.0%	% Earned Net Worth	27.0%
	53.7%	51.7%	21.9%	20.6%	18.9%	31.9%	35.5%	30.3%	NMF	14.1%	29.6%	31.0%	% Retained to Comm Eq	27.0%
	..	..	..	..	..	..	..	..	..	..	..	Nil	% All Div'ds to Net Prof	Nil

BUSINESS: Oracle Systems Corp. is the world's largest maker of database management systems (DBMS), software that allows users to create, retrieve, and manipulate data in computer-based files. Main products support ORACLE, a relational DBMS, which allows people to manipulate and retrieve data by requesting it using an industry-standard, English-like command language known as SQL. 1993 revenues: license fees, 60%; training & services, 40%. '93 depreciation rate, 20.3%. Foreign sales: 62%, profits 34%. R&D: 9.5% of sales. Has 9,245 empls., 2,500 stockholders. Insiders own 33% of stock (9/92 proxy). Chairman: James Abrahamson; President & C.E.O.: Lawrence J. Ellison. Inc.: DE. Add.: 500 Oracle Parkway, Redwood City, CA 94065. Tel.: 415-506-7000.

It's important to realize that short selling situations can turn into long positions, both of which can be profitable to the patient investor. See Figure 8–3, Oracle Systems Corporation.

Short selling presents ample opportunities to earn exceptional investment returns, but only if you do your homework. Don't get caught on the short end unless you know what you are doing.

.

9

warrants

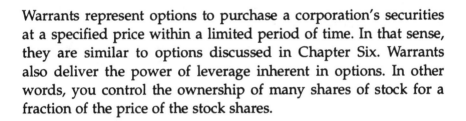

Warrants represent options to purchase a corporation's securities at a specified price within a limited period of time. In that sense, they are similar to options discussed in Chapter Six. Warrants also deliver the power of leverage inherent in options. In other words, you control the ownership of many shares of stock for a fraction of the price of the stock shares.

THE WARRANT ADVANTAGE

Warrants convey the right to purchase a specified number of stock shares, bonds, and sometimes other types of other securities. If you anticipate stock prices are poised to rise, it's wise to take a close look at the advantages of investing in this unique security.

As stock prices rise, the prices of warrants associated with the underlying security follow in suit. The real beauty of warrants is that you can control substantially more stock with a relatively smaller investment. This leverage capability enables you to compound your returns. A 10 percent surge in the price of the underlying stock could translate into a 40 percent jump in the price of the related warrant.

Another plus, your risk is limited to the "premium," or cost of the warrants you purchase. No matter how much the price of the underlying stock decreases, you can lose no more than the warrant premium.

Properly evaluating the opportunities in warrant investing must take into account the risks involved. The risk of investing in warrants stems from two major factors. First of all, their price changes correspond, for the most part, to changes in price levels of the underlying security. If the market price of the underlying security fails to rise, your warrants will also exhibit little profit opportunities.

Second, since warrants possess a limited lifespan, you run the risk that they will expire worthless before the price moves enough to generate a profit. However, while call options typically have life-spans of only a few months, warrants exist for a period of years, providing more opportunity for investment gains.

Warrant Terminology

Understanding a few basic terms in warrant investing is crucial. Learn the following definitions and how they impact your warrant investment decisions.

- **At the money.** The equilibrium point at which the exercise price and the price of the underlying security are equal. For example, a warrant with an exercise price of $15 and a current underlying security market price of 15 is "at the money." See intrinsic value.

- **Conversion option.** The right to convert the warrant into a specified number of units of the underlying security by paying a specified amount of money. This conversion must take place before the expiration date.

- **Exercise or "strike" price.** The price at which the warrant holder can exercise or purchase the underlying security.

- **Expiration date.** The last date by which the warrant can be exercised. While some perpetual warrants have been issued, the majority of warrants have limited life spans.

- **In the money.** The situation when the price of the underlying security is above the exercise price. For example, a warrant with an exercise price of $10 and with the stock price trading at $12 per share is "in the money." See intrinsic value.

- **Intrinsic value.** The difference between the exercise price and the stock price. For example, if the stock price is above the exercise price, the warrant possesses intrinsic value and said to be "in the money." In other words, the warrant can be exchanged for stock with a gain based on the difference between the two. More likely, the holder continues to hold the warrant and participates in the stock price rise with an upward movement in the warrant price. A warrant with the underlying stock price below the exercise price is without any intrinsic value and said to be "out of the money."

- **Naked.** The description of a warrant that has been issued independently of any underlying security.

- **Out of the money.** The situation when the warrant exercise price is above the price of the underlying security. For example, a warrant with an exercise price of $10 and an underlying stock market price of $8 per share is "out of the money." See intrinsic value.

- **Premium.** The market price or cost of the warrant. Also used to refer to the speculative value of the warrant; in other words, the difference between the current price of the underlying security and the warrant's intrinsic value. This premium fluctuates in relation to the price of the underlying security, investor sentiments toward future price movements, and the time remaining before the warrant expiration date. For example, if the warrant is "at the money," it has no intrinsic value. Now, if that same warrant trades for $1.50, that reflects the premium over intrinsic value. In another situation, if the underlying security trades at $15, the exercise price is $14 per share, and the warrant trades at $2, then the warrant has an intrinsic value of $1 and a premium of $1.

■ **Strike price.** See exercise price.

■ **Usable.** Indicates the condition when a debt security can be applied at face value instead of cash while exercising warrants. However, cash may be required in addition to the debt security.

■ **Warrant.** A security issued by a corporation that allows holders to purchase a specified amount of equity, debt, or other security at a specified price during a limited time span.

Your Own Stock Option Plan

We have all heard of corporate executives receiving lucrative stock options, the right to purchase the company's stock for a specified time frame at a guaranteed price. Warrants work in the same way, the major difference being that you have to pay for the warrant while corporate executives get this privilege as a condition of their corporate position, and hopefully, their exceptional performance.

More than 500 warrants trade on the New York Stock Exchange, American Stock Exchange, and over-the-counter markets. The stock tables typically indicate a warrant with the designation "wt" following the company name.

You need to thoroughly investigate before you invest in warrants, even more than you would for the underlying common stock. If you make a mistake in a common stock purchase and the price does not move upward as anticipated, you have time to wait for the price rise. However, since the warrant comes with a limited time span during which you can exercise your purchase option, you don't have the luxury of waiting a long time for the price move.

Factors to consider in the investment decision-making process include the prospects of the underlying company in terms of revenue and earnings potential, the firm's overall industry outlook, anticipated stock market moves, the expiration price in relation to the market price of the underlying security, the premium commanded by the warrant, the volatility of the underlying security's market price, and the time remaining until the warrant expiration date.

Remember, at no time do you risk more than you have invested in the warrant premium. But this investment premium leverages your ability to earn substantially higher investment gains.

It works like this. Assume that XYZ Corporation currently trades at $10 per share but you can purchase a warrant to purchase common shares of XYZ at an exercise price of $12 per share any time during the next five years. The cost for this privilege or premium of the warrant amounts to $1.

Now, if XYZ earns significantly higher earnings and its stock price jumps $5 per share to $15 per share, shareholders would have earned a 50 percent investment gain ($5/$10). Compare that return to the investment gain earned by an investor using the lever-age of warrants.

When the stock price rose $5 to $15 per share, the warrant price could have risen to $3 from the original $1 price. That's a 200 percent gain.

In addition to providing tremendous upside potential, warrants also help limit downside risk compared to owning the stock outright. To illustrate, assume instead of an upward stock price movement, the market price of XYZ Corporation shares declined from $10 per share to $5 per share. That's a 50 percent decline in value and a $5 loss per share.

On the other hand, if warrants were purchased for $1 and their premium declined to 25 cents, a higher percentage decline would have resulted (75 percent) but the money value loss, 75 cents, would be substantially less than that suffered by owning shares of XYZ stock.

You may be wondering, "Sure that works great in theory but how does it work in the real world?"

In my book, *Stock Picking* (McGraw-Hill, 1993) on pages 149–151, I used Tiger International as a prime example of a turn-around candidate and attractive convertible bond investment. Tiger also serves as a wonderful example of how to capitalize on the use of warrants.

In mid-1986, the air freight carrier was on the verge of crashing. Its stock price had already collapsed, plummeting from nearly $12 per share in mid-1983 to $3 5/8 per share in 1986. Simultaneously, a Tiger International warrant traded at 43 3/4 cents on the Pacific Stock Exchange.

To make a long story short, Tiger International, under the helm of Stephen Wolf, masterminded an incredible comeback, rising like a phoenix. Within a year, Wolf turned the air carrier around with earnings of $1.61 per share in 1987 versus a year earlier loss of $1.45 per share. By mid-1987, Tiger's stock price surged to $15 per share, a better than 300 percent performance. Not a bad return on your money.

However, investors savvy enough to purchase Tiger International warrants came out far better, earning nearly a 1,000 percent return on their investment as the price of the warrants jumped to $4 3/4.

An example of the use of warrants that did not pan out so well is Navistar International Corporation. Back in October, 1988 Navistar's stock traded around $5 1/8 per share. After a string of huge losses in the early 1980s and an improvement to 33 cents per share earnings in 1987, earnings were expected to nearly double in 1988.

At the time, Navistar had three outstanding warrant issues: "A" warrants allowed the holder to purchase a share of Navistar common stock for $5 per share, "B" warrants allowed the holder to buy Navistar common stock for $9 per share, and "C" warrants permitted the holder to purchase Navistar common stock for $7 per share.

There was still plenty of time to wait for Navistar management to turn the company around. Back in 1988, the "A" warrants traded at $2 1/8, "B" at $1, and "C" at $1 1/2.

Time was a crucial factor in the decision to purchase Navistar warrants. As it turned out, earnings did nearly double in 1988 to 64 cents per share. The firm's stock price rose to a 1989 high of $6 7/8 per share. Then things took another turn for the worse. Earnings declined in 1989 to 10 cents per share and the company suffered losses in 1990 through 1992 in the wake of an industry-wide downturn in truck sales.

Unfortunately, the "B" warrants expired on December 31, 1990, and the "C" warrants expired on December 4, 1992.

An upturn in the truck market resulted in projections of Navistar expecting to earn a profit in 1993. The company did a 1-for-10 reverse split on the company stock on July 1, 1993. Ten "A" warrants are now exchangeable for one share of Navistar Common stock at the exercise price of $50 per share. With the stock only trading around $26 1/4 per share in mid-August and the warrants due to expire on December 15, 1993, there did not appear much chance the warrants would prove to have any value and would expire worthless. At the time, they traded at 5/32 mainly due to the fact that the company could extend the "A" warrants' expiration date to December 15, 1999. See Figure 9–1, Navistar International Corporation.

Corporate Reasons for Warrant Issues

Warrants come about for a variety of reasons. They are often called "sweeteners" because they are included as an added benefit to entice investors by making a security more salable. Typi-

Figure 9–1
NAVISTAR INTERNATIONAL CORPORATION

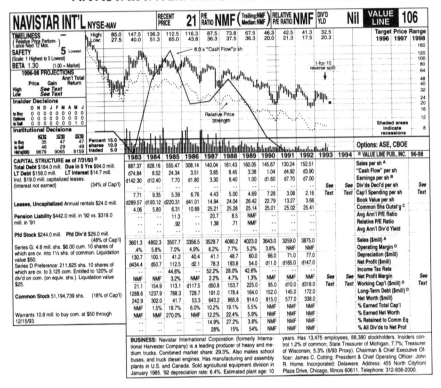

cally, the exercise price of the warrant is above the underlying security's current market price; therefore, it possesses no intrinsic value. Its attraction is the opportunity for future gains.

From the corporate perspective, the use of warrants reduces the costs of financing. Warrants have been used for original corporate financings, acquisitions, mergers, and reorganizations. Likewise, they have been issued in conjunction with both equity and debt securities. Warrants conserve cash because there are no dividend or interest payments to be made from corporate coffers.

On top of that, the use of warrants helps improve the corporate balance sheet since they don't raise debt levels or impact critical financial leverage and debt ratios.

Warrant Characteristics

Warrants are negotiable securities just like stocks and bonds. They are traded on organized exchanges and over-the-counter. But there is a major difference that investors must clearly understand before purchasing warrants. Unlike their stock and bond counterparts, warrants do not have any claim to dividend or interest payments, do not possess voting rights, and do not have any rights in the sale or liquidation of company assets.

In addition, warrant holders could suffer dilution if the issuer declares stock dividends, stock splits, or distributes common stock in other ways below the exercise price of the warrant.

As discussed earlier, most warrants have limited lives, usually expressed in a number of years. However, the terms of various warrants can change over time. For example, upward changes or "step-ups" in the exercise price, can result in a warrant having an initial exercise price of $10 per share, eventually moving up $1 to $11 per after a year and $12 per share after a second year. A "step-down" or decrease in the exercise price is also possible but occurs less frequently. These term changes are clearly spelled out in the warrant clauses and should be studied carefully.

Often the issuer can extend the life of the warrant, thereby, altering the original terms. The issuer could also declare debt securities to be usable at face value in place of cash. If the debt security is trading at a 50 percent discount to face value, the result is a substantial "step-down" in the exercise price of the warrant.

Know the warrant terms and possible scenarios which could impact the value of your warrant holdings. Forewarned is forearmed.

OTHER INVESTMENT FACTORS TO CONSIDER

In addition to warrant terms and scenarios such as exercise price, "step-ups," and dilution possibilities, it's important to recognize and consider other factors crucial to the proper warrant investment decision.

You must realize that warrant prices are volatile in comparison to the price of the underlying security. Price swings will be noticeably more erratic and volatile. This volatility provides the opportunity to substantially enhance your investment returns, but it can work to your disadvantage during downturns.

Like all investments, the laws of supply and demand come into play. Therefore, knowing the outstanding float of any particular warrant issue can work in your favor. Thinly traded warrants are characterized by large spreads between bid and ask prices and may be hard to liquidate when you want without taking a beating. Don't take the amount of float at face value. Investigate the owners of outstanding warrants. If the bulk of the float is in the hands of insiders unlikely to sell, the "real" float may be small with unwelcome consequences for your ability to trade and make a profit.

This small float can also pay big dividends if you are on the right side of the investment equation when heavy demand for the warrant pushes its price skyward.

Without a doubt, knowing the company, its industry, and future prospects ranks as the single best way to properly evaluate a warrant. Request copies of the firm's annual reports and 10Ks. Additional research sources such as *The Value Line Investment Survey* and *Standard & Poor's Stock Reports* are handy references you can find at your local library.

For publications specializing in investment information on warrants consult either *The R.H.M. Survey of Warrants Options & Low-Price Stocks* or *Value Line Convertibles*, which includes coverage of certain warrants.

The R.H.M. publication can be ordered from RHM Associates, 172 Forest Avenue, Glen Cove, New York 11542 or call 516-

759-2904. A full-year subscription for 50 issues costs $280 and a half-year subscription costs $150.

Recently, RHM did a review of the warrant recommendations it had made in its newsletter since September 1, 1991. As a whole, the nine warrants recommended for purchase were up an average 64 percent. According to the newsletter, the boom in new stock offerings, often accompanied by warrants, and a noticeable uptick in the issuance of warrants in general, in recent times, suggest stellar profit opportunities will continue to abound.

The Value Line publication comes out 48 times a year and can be purchased for $475 per year. Reduced period and rate trial offers are regularly advertised in *Barron's*, *The Wall Street Journal*, and *Investor's Business Daily*. You can order from Value Line Publishing Inc., 711 Third Avenue, New York 10017-4064 or call 212-687-3965.

Use the above information to ferret out turn-around situations or other mispriced stocks and their warrants for substantial investment performance. Look for market inequities or inefficiencies.

Using a long-term investing philosophy and buying on weakness in the underlying stock and warrant prices can pay off for the patient investor. The market often overreacts to news and then rebounds as the "facts" get sorted out. Use these opportunities to establish or increase your position in the warrant of a company well-positioned to rebound or capitalize on industry or economic events.

Since the amount of premium you pay for a warrant ultimately impacts your overall investment return, it is crucial to calculate the premium as a percentage of the common stock price. This helps you determine the excess cost of acquiring a share through the use of warrants.

Typically, the premium is noted as a percent of the common stock price. To calculate the premium, subtract the difference between the common stock price and the exercise price from the price of the warrant and divide by the common stock price.

$$\frac{WP - (SP - EP)}{SP} = \text{Premium \%}$$

EP = Exercise Price
SP = Stock Price
WP = Warrant Price

For a warrant with a $6 premium (price) on a stock trading at $35 per share and an exercise price of $30 per share, the warrant premium is calculated as follows:

$$\frac{6 - (35 - 30)}{35} = 2.8\%$$

In other words, acquiring the common stock through purchase and exercise of the warrants costs almost three percent more than purchasing the stock directly. You have to weigh the premium cost versus the benefits of using warrant leverage.

While the above calculation used a warrant that was already "in the money," the following example illustrates the premium calculation for a warrant "out of the money."

In this case, the warrant costs $2, the common stock price is $10, and the exercise price is $15 and results in a premium of 70 percent.

$$\frac{2 - (10 - 15)}{10} = 70\%$$

Other Warrant Strategies

You can use your knowledge gained in Chapter Eight, Short Selling, in the world of warrants. Just as you might decide to short a company's stock whose price you feel has good possibilities of starting or continuing a downward trend, you can also short sell the company's warrant.

The process works exactly the same. You borrow the security, in this case the warrant, from your broker and sell what you don't own with the anticipation that you can buy it back later at a price low enough to return the borrowed security, pay the interest and commission fees and make a profit.

You can reduce your risk posture by matching your warrant investment with a hedge. You might want to employ a hedge when you believe the purchase of a particular warrant is the right decision but would like to reduce your risk of owning a wasting asset (one that expires worthless at a given date).

This hedge can take the form of a combination of the purchase or sale of a warrant with an offsetting position in a related security. For example, you can hedge your short sale of an XYZ Corporation warrant with the purchase of the underlying common stock of XYZ Corporation. Or you can purchase the warrant and short the underlying common stock.

Another way of hedging involves purchasing warrants and selling options see Chapter Six, Options.

The Turnaround Letter recently highlighted using warrants to take advantage of companies emerging out of Chapter 11 bankruptcy protection. Many of these companies issue warrants as part of their corporate reorganizations.

Since these warrants will have no intrinsic value, their worth lies in the expectations of investors for better days ahead.

It's wise to search for warrants with small premiums (lower investment posture and risk) and a long time period left before expiration, giving the company's management ample time to work their magic and bring the firm back to prosperity with a corresponding rise in the company's stock and warrant prices.

To be sure, investing in post-bankruptcy warrants is not for the conservative investor. But for those aggressive investors seeking extraordinary returns, post-bankruptcy warrants offer several enticements in addition to the leverage inherent in all warrants.

First of all, the newly emerged companies tend to be neglected by Wall Street analysts, thus, creating the possibility of under-valued situations. Second, post-bankruptcy warrants, being relatively new, often carry an expiration date long into the future.

One post-bankruptcy warrant covered in the August 1993 issue that the *The Turnaround Letter* found particularly appealing was issued by National Convenience Stores.

The National Convenience warrants carried an exercise price of $17 3/4 while the common stock traded at $15 1/4 per share. With no intrinsic value, these warrants commanded a premium of $3 3/4. With an expiration date of March 9, 1998, an investor had more than five years for the stock price to rise enough over the exercise price to recover the premium and make a profit.

As a measure of the leverage in the National Convenience Stores warrant, the anticipated appreciation in the warrant price if the underlying stock price rose 50 percent is estimated at 37 percent. For a 100 percent rise in the stock price, the warrant appreciation surges to 240 percent.

The Turnaround Letter can be ordered from New Generation Research, Inc., Suite 801, 225 Friend Street, Boston, Massachusetts 02114, 617-573-9550. An annual subscription costs $195.

SOME FINAL NOTES ON WARRANT INVESTING

Investing in warrants takes investigative time and your attention. You must keep appraised of upcoming expiration dates and how they will impact the value of the warrant as that date approaches, finally expiring worthless if proper action is not taken.

Search out companies with dramatic upside potential and/or undervalued situations not yet appreciated by the overall market.

Used prudently, warrants can enhance your performance track record. Understand the risks and thoroughly investigate before investing.

10

zeroing in
on zeros

THE ZERO CONNECTION

Zero-coupon bonds appear confusing to many people. Traditional bonds earn interest and make periodic, typically semi-annual, interest payments to the bond owners. For example, assume you purchase a $1,000 bond with an annual coupon interest rate of eight percent. Every six months, you will receive an interest payment of $40 [(1,000 × .08) /2].

The zero coupon, on the other hand, works a bit differently. Your investment still earns interest but you do not receive any interest payments over the life of the bond. Instead, you purchase the bond at a discount, say $200, and it compounds to mature at a future specified date with a value of $1,000.

One of the beauties of the zero-coupon bond is that you don't need $1,000 to start your investment. Small minimum investments can combine to build quite a nest egg at yields higher than those obtainable from bank savings accounts and certificates of deposit.

U.S. TREASURY GUARANTEE

Assuming the zero coupon is a U.S. Treasury zero-coupon bond, you also have safety of principal through a U.S. government guarantee. Contrary to what many people mistakenly believe, and this is extremely important to understand, this government guarantee does not warrant your investment safe from market or interest rate risk.

Zero-coupon bonds, like other bonds, will fluctuate in value depending on changes in interest rates, investor sentiment, and other economic factors. In other words, your zero coupon could be worth $750 today and only $700 next week if market interest rates jump sharply.

The government guarantee applies to the maturity value of the bond. In other words, Uncle Sam guarantees to payoff the established maturity value, $1,000 in the example above, upon maturity. In the meantime, the value of the zero-coupon bond is free to fluctuate upward and downward in response to interest rate and other market pressures.

Another benefit of using zeros to build a sizable nest egg stems from their ability to side step interest reinvestment risk to a degree. As your zero earns interest, it is automatically reinvested at the interest rate locked in when you purchased the bond. If you bought a zero-coupon bond with an interest rate of eight percent and a maturity date in the year 2020, you will continue to earn that eight percent rate even if market interest rates drop to two percent in the meantime.

You also avoid the situation of trying and failing to reinvest interest proceeds. If you receive a $40 interest check, what do you do with it? Chances are you spend it because you need at least $1,000 to purchase a certificate of deposit. Even if you do save the $40 by placing it into a money market account or bank savings account, the interest rate you earn will probably trail that offered by zero-coupon bonds. In comparison, interest earned on zero-coupon bonds automatically gets reinvested and compound to earn the stated rate of interest.

Zeros also help with your long-term financial planning. You know upfront how much money you will receive upon maturity. As long as you hold the zero-coupon bonds to maturity, the guess work is completely eliminated. This dependability factor makes zeros excellent investment vehicles for establishing funds to meet college or retirement expenses.

If you do decide to sell your U.S. Treasury zero-coupon bonds before maturity, an active secondary market helps ensure their liquidity. Of course, the value of the bonds will depend on current interest rate levels and market conditions.

Since U.S. Treasury zero-coupon bonds are direct obligations of the U.S. government they represent the highest quality (lowest risk) investments available. As federal government securities, interest earned on U.S. Treasury zero-coupon bonds is free from state income taxes. This last feature is kind of a mute point, however, as we shall soon see.

PHANTOM INCOME

That leads us to another important feature of zero-coupon bonds. The interest earned on the bonds is fully taxable even though you don't receive any of it until maturity. You must report this "phantom income" on your annual income tax return and pay taxes accordingly. Obviously, this is a major disadvantage.

You can circumvent the "phantom income" tax by investing in zero-coupon bonds within tax-sheltered accounts such as individual retirement accounts (IRAs), custodial accounts, or other types of retirement accounts.

Like all fixed income investments, you need to assess the probable future interest rate environment when deciding on the length of maturities. Zero-coupon bonds yielded an enviable 19.8 percent in 1991 in the wake of dropping interest rates. Today, with interest rates at historic lows, the odds are that market interest rates will rise before going lower. Under that scenario, it would be foolish to place a lot of money in zero-coupon bonds, or any other bonds for that matter, with maturity dates too far into the future.

If you can live with the current level of interest rates and like the assurance of receiving a set sum in the future, you can take a longer term investment position. After all, the U.S. government does guarantee the maturity value of these zeros. The same does not hold true for corporate zero-coupon bonds or for municipal zero-coupon bonds. In those cases, you will have to assume more risk.

The zero coupon concept should not be too foreign or confusing to you. If you ever owned a U.S. savings bond, in effect, you owned a zero-coupon bond without knowing it. Savings bonds were purchased at a discount and earned interest to a maturity value set in advance. It's that simple.

Using Table 10–1, Market Value of Zero-Coupon Bonds, we can see how changing interest rates impact the market value of a zero-coupon bond.

Table 10–1
MARKET VALUE OF ZERO-COUPON BONDS

Years to Maturity	Yield to Maturity				
	5%	6%	7%	8%	9%
30	$227	$170	$127	$ 95	$ 71
25	290	228	179	141	111
20	372	307	253	208	172
16	454	388	333	285	244
10	610	554	503	456	415
5	781	744	709	676	644
1	952	943	933	925	916

Assume you purchase a 20-year zero-coupon bond at seven percent for $253. In four years it would be worth $333, assuming interest rates don't change. Now if interest rates drop to five percent in four years, the zero coupon would command a value of $454. On the other hand, if market interest rates rose to nine percent at the end of four years, the zero-coupon bond would be worth only $244, or less than you paid for it.

Of course, you can play the interest game for higher overall returns and cash in with an attractive profit if rates decline as you anticipate. Even if interest rates do go against you and rise, causing the market value of your zero coupon to decline, you can still hold the bond to maturity and receive your guaranteed rate of interest all along the way. Remember, the federal government guarantees the principal maturity amount on U.S. Treasury zero-coupon bonds.

Dollar cost averaging your zero purchases can help hedge against interest rate risk and rising inflation rates. Or you can ladder your purchases with different maturity dates to eliminate all of your investments coming due at once and risking having to reinvest at much lower yields.

For those wishing to trade in zero-coupon bonds and not hold them to maturity, it's important to remember that zeros tend to react with more volatility than other bonds. Since zero-coupon bonds pay no current interest income which can be reinvested at higher yields if market interest rates increase, the market value of existing zeros will decline more rapidly. On the plus side, if interest rates decline, the market value of zeros will move more faster and farther on the upside.

For example, The Benham Target 2020 Fund will rise 33 percent for every one-percentage-point drop in long-term Treasury rates and will fall 25 percent for each one-percentage-point jump in those rates while the Benham Target 2015 will move up 27 percent and decline 21 percent for the same percentage point shifts. The longer to maturity, the more the price swing.

CHAPTER TEN

LYONS, TIGRS, CATS, STRIPS, ETC.

LYONS and TIGRS and . . . no this isn't Auntie Em and Dorothy. Since the Treasury does not issue zeros directly to the investing public, you have to purchase them through your broker in the form of packaged zeros. Actually, STRIPS are direct issues of the U.S. government but they are not issued by the U.S. government and private investors can't buy them. Sounds like governmentese to me. Anyway, each brokerage firm has its own name and acronym for its brand of zeros thus, the LYONS and TIGRS . . . .

Incidentally, LYONS, TIGRS, CATS, AND STRIPS stand for Liquid Yield Option Notes, Treasury Investment Growth Receipts, Certificates of Accrual on Treasury Securities, and Separate Trading of Registered Interest and Principal of Securities.

Since the underlying zero-coupon bonds of these instruments are U.S. Treasury zero-coupon bonds, they still carry the same government guarantee of maturity amount.

Unfortunately, bid/ask spreads can take a chunk out of your zero coupon profit possibilities. For a bond trading at $190 per $1,000 face value, the spread could approach three percent. You can get around this expense by purchasing your zeros the mutual fund way. Scudder's Zero Coupon 2000 Fund (1-800-225-2470) and Benham's Target Maturities Funds (1-800-472-3389) specialize in the zero coupon field and charge no load fees. Investors can open a Benham Target Fund IRA for as little as $100 and Benham does not charge an annual maintenance fee on its IRA accounts.

ZERO-COUPON MUNICIPAL BONDS

These zeros are issued by state and local government jurisdictions to raise money for public purposes such as sewer systems, schools, and public buildings. Interest earned on municipal securities is exempt from federal income taxes (with the exception of the alternative minimum tax calculation) and in some cases also exempt from state and local income tax. Obviously, their tax-exempt status makes municipal zero-coupon bonds more acceptable for non-tax-sheltered investment accounts.

Of course, you would have to compare the yield on a tax-exempt municipal security with that offered by a similar quality taxable investment to see which makes more sense in your financial and tax situation. Table 10–2, Tax-Exempt/Taxable Yield Equivalents, provides a comparison for different income levels.

Table 10–2
TAX-EXEMPT/TAXABLE YIELD EQUIVALENTS

Taxable Income	Fed Tax	4.00%	5.00%	5.5%	6.00%	6.5%
			Equivalent Taxable Yields*			
Single Return						
To $22,100	15%	4.71	5.88	6.47	7.06	7.65
$22,101–$53,500	28	5.56	6.94	7.64	8.33	9.03
Over $53,500	31	5.80	7.25	7.97	8.70	9.42
Joint Return						
To $36,900	15	4.71	5.88	6.47	7.06	7.65
$36,901–$89,150	28	5.56	6.94	7.64	8.33	9.03
Over $89,150	31	5.80	7.25	7.97	8.70	9.42

Tax-Free Yields shown as column header over the 4.00%, 5.00%, 5.5%, 6.00%, 6.5% columns.

* Based on rates and taxable income in effect January 1, 1993

In the wake of the Tax Reform Act of 1986, municipal zero-coupon bonds have surfaced as one of few remaining investments with tax-favored status, thus making them very popular with investors.

When considering to invest in municipal zero-coupon bonds, it's imperative to assess the credit quality of the issuing body and the how and from where repayment of the debt will materialize. Since your maturity value is established in advance, your only risk to principal, if you don't sell your zero-coupon bonds before maturity, lies in default by the issuing body.

The strongest municipal guarantee comes in the form of a general obligation security backed by the taxing power of the state or other jurisdiction issuing the zero coupon. Funds to repay the debt derive from specified taxes or fees collected, such as highway tolls or special sales tax levies.

Bonds backed by specific revenue generating projects such as sewer systems and highways are termed project bonds. The accreted interest is paid out of revenues financed by the capital borrowed. Since these project zeros need to generate money before investors can be repaid, they are considered less financially secure investments than those backed by the taxing authority of the issuing jurisdiction.

Independent rating agencies assess the ability of municipal zero-coupon bonds issuers to repay their debt, assigning ratings indicating the relative safety against default of each specific issue. Fitch Investor's Service, Inc., Moody's Investor Service, and Standard & Poor's Corporation review and analyze the jurisdiction's financial standing and debt coverage capabilities for a particular issue to give it an investment grade.

Issues with the maximum assurance against default rate the highest or AAA rating. For example, top quality issues earn a AAA rating as do "escrowed" zeros, those in which the issuer has purchased U.S. government bonds or deposited compensating balances in a depositary bank to act as collateral for the municipal zero coupon debt. Insured municipal bonds, with a financial guarantee of additional backing to ensure repayment of principal and interest, also can garner a AAA rating.

Lower ratings such as AA an A still represent quality issues but with less protection against possible default occurring. Zero-coupon bonds rated BBB represent the lowest "investment grade" securities.

You have to weigh your own investment goals and the risk posture you are comfortable assuming, but as a general rule, conservative investors should stick with A or above ratings on municipal zeros and AA for long-term investments. As in other types of investments, higher quality issues typically carry lower interest rates and vice versa.

Municipal zero-coupon bonds often come with a call feature. This means the issuer can redeem the zero before maturity after a certain date and under certain conditions. Clearly, this call feature can impact the overall yield you actually end up receiving on your investment.

To illustrate, assume you purchase a municipal zero coupon with an interest rate of eight percent. If interest rates decline substantially after the issue date, it would make sense for the issuing jurisdiction to call or retire the bonds, in terms with the call provisions, in order to eliminate high cost debt and replace it with other debt paying lower interest rates. If the zero-coupon bonds are called, your investment, which had been earning eight percent, will have to be reinvested, most likely at substantially lower yields.

Make sure you know the call provisions and how they can impact your anticipated yield. Municipal coupon bonds paying the same stated interest rate and maturing at the same time could possess radically different call provisions. It pays to check out the fine print.

For example, one municipal zero-coupon bond could be callable after two years of issue by paying 102 percent of compound accreted value while another otherwise similar municipal might not be callable until after five years of issue and paying 105 percent of compound accreted value, thus providing substantially longer interest rate protection and a much higher retirement payoff.

Typically, municipal zeros are not callable until five or ten years after issue so the time remaining to the call date becomes the critical issue.This time period to call date is termed call protection.

Even if your issue is recalled, it may not affect you. Some recalls may not be for the entire issue but instead recall the zeros based on their serial number. Don't depend on the luck of the draw. Try to obtain yield to call that remains competitive with yield to maturity so your investment return will not be significantly hurt by a municipal zero-coupon bond recall.

You need to factor in the stated interest rate, call provisions, maturity date, yield to maturity, yield to call date, issue investment grade rating, your investment goals, and risk tolerance into your decision making process in order to choose the proper investment for you.

The popularity of municipal zero-coupon bonds to investors is evidenced in the amount issued each year. For each of the three years in the period from 1990 through 1992, more than $4 billion in zero coupon municipals hit the streets and were gobbled up by investors large and small.

Government talk of raising marginal personal income tax rates and eliminating even more tax shelters promises to make the tax-exempt municipal zero-coupon bond even more enticing to middle-income and above investors in the future.

Innovations in the zero-coupon bond field in recent years include the convertible zero coupon municipal bond. They work like this. The bonds start their lives as zero-coupon bonds and after a stated period of time, generally 8 to 15 years, convert to interest paying bonds.

The main attraction is for investors nearing retirement. They can earn interest tax sheltered until retirement, then receive the interest stream in cash to enhance their retirement cash flow to meet anticipated living expenses.

Another variation of the municipal zero-coupon bond comes in the form of stripped municipals. In this case, these municipals pay interest semiannually via coupons which are stripped from the bond. The bond still sells at a deep discount from face value.

THE CORPORATE ZERO

Governments are not alone in finding out that investors like the benefits offered by zero-coupon bonds. A number of corporations have also gone the zero coupon route to raise capital. In many cases, companies have innovatively combined the attributes of the straight zero-coupon bond with a convertibility feature, making the issue even more attractive to investors. See Chapter Three,

Captivating Convertibles, for an in-depth discussion of the attributes of convertible securities.

For example, in 1990, Illinois Tool Works Inc. (NYSE: ITW) issued $250 million maturity value of zero coupon convertible subordinated debentures due in the year 2005. The debentures were convertible into common stock of Illinois Tool Works, or at the option of the company, into cash equal to the value of the common stock upon conversion.

Likewise, Walt Disney Company (NYSE: DIS) tapped the corporate zero coupon market with an issue of $1.5 billion of zero-coupon bonds due in the year 2005. The bonds were convertible into cash equal to the market price of Euro Disneyland S.C.A. shares, a publicly traded French firm established to build and operate Euro Disneyland in France.

The Disney issue accomplished several firsts. Disney was the largest company to raise capital by issuing convertible zero-coupon bonds, the offering was the largest single convertible issue up to that time, and the issue represented the first time U.S. investors purchased a security convertible into the cash equivalent of the price of a foreign stock.

The Disney zeros took on the LYONs (Liquid Yield Option Notes) designation of zeros underwritten by the Merrill Lynch Capital Markets unit. They will pay a yield of six percent to maturity and offer the upside appreciation potential of the stock price of Euro Disneyland S.C.A.

The Disney convertible zeros were issued at a discount price of $412 per $1,000 of maturity value and can be converted at any time at a premium of 15 percent to the price of Euro Disneyland S.C.A. stock on the day the bonds were issued.

The real attraction of the zero-coupon convertible bond lies in the investor's ability to participate in the upside potential of the underlying stock while maintaining a desired yield and possibly a tax-sheltered income if the investment is in an IRA or other tax-sheltered vehicle.

You can take an aggressive stance with long-term zero coupons, if you anticipate interest rates dropping in the future. In addition to earning your locked-in yield, you have the opportunity for substantial capital gains as the market value of existing zeros react to lower interest rates.

GOVERNMENT AGENCY ZEROS

There's a bevy of zero-coupon bonds issued by government agencies such as the Federal National Mortgage Association (FNMA or Fannie Mae), the Government National Mortgage Association (Ginnie Mae), Student Loan Marketing Association, and even the Tennessee Valley Authority among others.

These agency zeros are not always backed by a government guarantee so check out the fine print. In other words, they may not be direct financial obligations of the federal government and thus carry a higher risk posture than those backed by the government. Even so, many of these zeros sport AAA ratings.

In the August/September 1991 issue of *Your Money*, I featured a new entry into the zero market, the government-agency accrual zeros. These unique bonds were to mature at a set figure after a period of years, just like other zeros; however, they then went on to pay 9.5 percent interest for the remaining six years of their life.

In comparison to U.S. Treasuries, the accrual Z's paid a higher yield, partly because they were a tad below Treasuries in terms of quality but also because the market did not quite understand them yet, making for inefficient pricing.

You could have purchased $75,000 worth of FNMA July 5, 2014 accrual Z's for around $10,000 in mid-May, 1991. By the end of December, 1991, those zeros were worth around $11,000, for a 10 percent gain in a little over six months.

Now, if you held onto those accrual Z's until mid-August 1993, they would have been worth nearly $17,500, a 75 percent gain in a bit over two years.

With an initial yield just under nine percent, the market value of these accrual Z's surged when interest rates went on a steady decline over that time frame.

That profitable advice came from Herbert Davidson, senior vice president with Meyers, Pollock, Robbins, Inc. based in McClean, Virginia.

Today, Davidson still finds accrual Z's a good investment for those investors seeking long-term wealth building but warns that zeros are not for the conservative investor due to their volatility.

Investigate zero coupon investments that meet your investment goals and risk parameters.

glossary

ACCRETED The process of earning or growing gradually. For example, the interest on zero coupon bonds is accreted.

ADJUSTABLE RATE PREFERRED A preferred security with its dividend payment pegged to a specific index or indices.

AMERICAN DEPOSITARY RECEIPT (ADR) A negotiable receipt for shares of a foreign corporation held in the vault of a United States depositary bank.

ANNUAL REPORT The Securities and Exchange Commisssion-required report presenting a portrayal of the company's operations and financial position. It includes a balance sheet, income statement, statement of cash flows, description of company operations, management discussion of company financial condition and operating results and any events which materially impact the company.

ASSET ALLOCATION   Investment strategy of reducing risk and increasing return by investing in a variety of asset types.

ASSET PLAY   A stock investment that value investors find attractive due to asset undervaluation by the market.

AT THE MONEY   The situation when the underlying security's market price equals the exercise price.

BASIS PRICE   The cost of an investment used to determine capital gains or losses.

BEAR MARKET   A period of time during which stock prices decline over a period of months or years.

BOND   A long-term debt security which obligates the issuer to pay interest and repay the principal. The holder does not have any ownership rights in the issuer.

BOND RATIO   The measure of a company's leverage comparing the firm's debt to total capital.

BOTTOM UP INVESTING   Investment strategy starting with company fundamentals and then moving to the overall economic and investment environment.

BUSTED   A convertible whose underlying common stock value has fallen so low that the convertible provision no longer holds any value.

CALL OPTION   A contract providing the holder the right to buy the underlying security at a specific price during a specified time period.

CALL PROVISION   A provision allowing the security issuer to recall the security before maturity.

CASH EQUIVALENT   Asset type with maturities of less than one year.

CASH FLOW   The flow of funds in and out of an operating business. Normally calculated as net income plus depreciation and other noncash items.

CASH FLOW/DEBT RATIO   The relationship of free cash flow to total long-term indebtedness. This ratio is helpful in tracking a firm's ability to meet scheduled debt and interest payment requirements.

CASH FLOW/INTEREST RATIO   This ratio determines how many times free cash flow will cover fixed interest payments on long-term debt.

CASH FLOW PER SHARE   Cash flow per share represents the amount earned before deduction for depreciation and other charges not involving the outlay of cash.

CASH RATIO   This ratio is used to measure liquidity. It is calculated as the sum of cash and marketable securities divided by current liabilities. It indicates how well a company can meet current liabilities.

CLOSED-END FUND   An investment fund with a fixed number of shares outstanding and trades on exchanges like stock in regular companies.

CLUSTER INVESTING   Method of diversification recommending investing in stocks from different clusters or groups.

COMMON AND PREFERRED CASH FLOW COVERAGE RATIOS   These ratios determine how many times annual free cash flow will cover common and preferred cash dividend payments.

COMMON STOCK RATIO   The relationship of common stock to total company capitalization.

CONTRARIAN   An investor seeking securities out-of-favor with other investors.

CONVERTIBLE   A security that is exchangeable into common stock at the option of the holder under specified terms and conditions.

COVERED CALL   An option in which the investor owns the underlying security.

CUMULATIVE   As it relates to preferred stock, any unpaid preferred dividends accrue and must be paid prior to resumption of common stock dividends.

CURRENT RATIO   Liquidity ratio calculated by dividing current assets by current liabilities.

CYCLES   Repeating patterns of business, economic, and market activity.

CYCLICAL   Industries and companies that advance and decline in relation to the changes in the overall economic environment.

DEBT-TO-EQUITY RATIO   The relationship of debt to shareholder's equity in a firm's capitalization structure.

DEFENSIVE INVESTMENTS   Securities that are less affected by economic contractions, thus offering downside price protection.

DIVERSIFICATION   The spreading of investment risk by owning different types of securities, investments in different geographical markets, etc.

DOLLAR COST AVERAGING Investment strategy of investing a fixed amount of money over time to achieve a lower average security purchase price.

DOW JONES INDUSTRIAL AVERAGE Market index consisting of 30 U.S. industrial companies. Used as a measure of market performance.

DOW THEORY Investment theory that the market moves in three simultaneous movement which help forecast the direction of the economy and the market.

DRIP Dividend reinvestment plan in which stockholder can purchase additional shares with dividends and/or cash.

EARNINGS PER SHARE Net after tax income divided by the number of outstanding company shares.

ECONOMIC SERIES The complete cycle of types of economic periods such as from expansion to slowdown to contraction to recession/depression to increased activity back to expansion.

ECONOMIC VALUE The economic value of a stock represents the anticipated free cash flow the company will generate over a period of time, discounted by the weighted cost of a company's capital.

EFFICIENT MARKET A market which instantly takes into account all known financial information and reflects it in the security's price.

EXERCISE PRICE The price at which an option of futures contract can be executed. Also known as the striking price.

EXPIRATION DATE The last day on which an option or future can be exercised.

FEDERAL RESERVE   The national banking system consisting of 12 independent federal reserve banks in Atlanta, Boston, Chicago, Cleveland, Dallas, Kansas City, Minneapolis, New York, Philadelphia, Richmond, St. Louis, and San Francisco.

FISCAL YEAR   The 12-month accounting period that conforms to the company's natural operating cycle versus the calendar year.

FREDDIE MAC   The nickname of the Federal Home Loan Mortgage Corporation.

FREE CASH FLOW   Free cash flow is determined by calculating operating earnings after taxes and then adding depreciation and other noncash expenses, less capital expenditures and increases in working capital.

FREE CASH FLOW/EARNINGS RATIO   The percentage of earnings actually available in cash. It is the percentage of free cash available to company management for investments, acquisitions, plant construction, dividends, etc.

FUNDAMENTAL ANALYSIS   Investment strategy focusing on the intrinsic value of the company as evidenced by a review of the balance sheet, income statement, cash flow, operating performance, etc.

GAP   The occurrence of a trading pattern when the price range from one day does not overlap the previous day's price range.

GLOBAL DEPOSITARY RECEIPT (GDR)   Similar to ADRs. Depositary receipt issued in the international community representing shares in a foreign company. Other designations include International Depositary Receipt (IDR) and European Depositary Receipt (EDR).

GROWTH INVESTMENTS Companies or industries with earnings projected to outpace the market consistently over the long-term.

HIGH-TECH STOCK Securities of firms in high-technology industries such as biotechnology, computers, electronics, lasers, medical devices, and robotics.

HYBRID SECURITY A security that possesses the characteristics of both stock and bonds, such as a convertible bond.

INDENTURE The legal contract spelling out the terms and conditions between the issuer and bondholders.

INDEX Compilation of performance for specific groupings of stocks or mutual funds such as the Dow Jones Industrial Average, S&P 500, etc.

INDICATOR A measurement of the economy or securities markets used by economists and investment analysts to predict future economic and financial moves and direction. Indicators are classifed as leading, coincidental, or lagging. Indicator examples include interest rate changes, utility consumption, number of unemployment claims, etc.

IPO (INITIAL PUBLIC OFFERING) The first public offering of a company's stock.

INSIDER Anyone having access to material corporate information. Most frequently used to refer to company officers, directors, and top management.

INSTITUTIONAL INVESTOR Investor organizations, such as pension funds and money managers, who trade large volumes of securities.

IN THE MONEY The situation when the price of the underlying security is above the exercise price.

INTRINSIC VALUE The difference between the current market price of the underlying security and the striking price of a related option.

JUNK BONDS Bonds with ratings below investment grade.

LEADING INDICATOR An economic measurement that tends to accurately predict the future direction of the economy or stock market.

LEAPS Long-term equity participation securities. Long-term options with maturities up to two years.

LEVERAGE The use of debt to finance a company's operations. Also, the use of debt by investors to increase the return on investment from securities transactions.

LIFE CYCLE INVESTING Developing an investment strategy based on where you are in your life cycle.

LIQUIDITY The degree of ease in which assets can be turned into readily available cash.

LISTED Investment securities that have met the listing requirements of a particular exchange.

MAINTENANCE MARGIN The minimum equity value that must be maintained in a margin account. Initial margin requirements include a minimum deposit of $2,000 before any credit can be extended. Current Regulation T rules require maintenance margin equal at least 50 percent of the market value of the margined positions.

MARGIN   The capital (in cash or securities) that an investor deposits with a broker to borrow additional funds to purchase securities.

MARGIN CALL   A demand from a broker for additional cash or securities as collateral to bring the margin account back within maintenance limits.

MUTUAL FUND   An investment company that sells shares in itself to the investing public and uses the proceeds to purchase individual securities.

NAFTA   North American Free Trade Agreement.

NAKED OPTION   An option written when the investor does not have a position in the underlying security.

NASDAQ   National Association of Securities Dealers Automated Quotation System providing computerized quotes of market makers for stocks traded over the counter.

NET ASSET VALUE   The quoted market value of a mutual fund share. Determined by dividing the closing market value of all securities owned by the mutual fund plus all other assets and liabilities by the total number of shares outstanding.

NUMISMATICS   The study, collection of, and investment in money and medals.

OPTION   A security that gives the holder the right to purchase or sell a particular investment at a fixed price for a specified period of time.

OUT OF THE MONEY   An option whose striking price is higher than the underlying security's current market price for a call option or whose striking price is lower than the current market price for a put option.

PARTICIPATING   As it relates to preferred stock, the preferred stockholder shares in additional dividends as the earnings of the company improve.

PAYOUT RATIO   The percentage of a company's profit paid out in cash dividends.

PORTFOLIO   The investment holdings of an individual or institutional investor, including stocks, bonds, options, money market accounts, etc.

PREFERRED   A security with preference to dividends and claim to corporate assets over common stock.

PRICE/EARNINGS RATIO   Determined by dividing the stock's market price by its earnings per common share. Used as an indicator of company performance and in comparison with other stock investments and the overall market.

PUT OPTION   A contract giving the holder the right to sell the underlying security at a specific price over a specified time frame.

QUICK RATIO   The quick ratio is used to measure corporate liquidity. It is regarded as an improvement over the current ratio which includes the usually not very liquid inventory. The quick ratio formula is computed as current assets less inventory divided by current liabilities.

RANGE   The high and low prices over which the security trades during a specific time frame; day, month, 52-weeks, etc.

RATING   Independent ranking of a security in regard to risk and ability to meet payment obligations.

REBALANCING   The process of adjusing a portfolio mix to return to a desired asset allocation level.

RELATIVE STRENGTH   Comparison of a security's earnings or stock price strength in relation to other investments or indices.

RISK   The financial uncertainty that the actual return will vary from the expected return. Risk factors include inflation, deflation, interest rate risk, market risk, liquidity, default, etc.

RULE OF EIGHT   Diversification strategy that contends a minimum of eight stocks is necessary to properly diversify a portfolio.

SECONDARY MARKET   Market where previously issued securities trade such as the New York Stock Exchange.

SHORT AGAINST THE BOX   Investment strategy of selling short while holding a long position in the security.

SHORT SALE   Sale of a security not yet owned in order to capitalize on an anticipated market price drop.

SHORT SQUEEZE   Rapid price rise forcing investors to cover their short positions. This drives the security price up even higher, often squeezing even more short investors.

SPECIAL SITUATION   An undervalued security with special circumstances such as management change, new product, technological breakthrough, etc., favoring its return to better operating performance and higher prices.

SPIN-OFF   Shedding of a corporate subsidiary, division, or other operation via the issuance of shares in the new corporate entity.

SPLIT   A change in the number of outstanding shares through board of directors' action. Shareholder's equity remains the same; each shareholder receives the new stock in proportion to their holdings on the date of record. Dividends and earnings per share are adjusted to reflect the stock split.

S&P 500 Broad-based stock index composed of 400 industrial, 40 financial, 40 utility, and 20 transportation stocks.

STRIKING PRICE The price at which an option or future contract can be executed according to the terms of the contract. Also called exercise price.

10K,10Q Annual and quarterly reports required by the Securities and Exchange Commission. They contain more in-depth financial and operating information than the annual and quarterly stockholder's reports.

TECHNICAL ANALYSIS Investment strategy that focuses on market and stock price patterns.

TOP-DOWN INVESTING Investment strategy starting with the overall economic scenario and then moving downward to consider industry and individual company investments.

TOTAL RETURN The return achieved by combining both the dividend/interest and capital appreciation earned on an investment.

TRADING RANGE The spread between the high and low prices for a given period.

TURNAROUND A positive change in the fortunes of a company or industry. Turnarounds occur for a variety of reasons such as economic upturn, new management, new product lines, strategic acquisition, etc.

UNDERLYING SECURITY The security which may be bought or sold under the terms of an option agreement, warrant, etc.

UNDERVALUED SITUATION A security with a market value that does not fully value its potential or the true value of the company.

UPTREND   Upward movement in the market price of a stock.

VOLUME   The number of units of a security traded during a given time frame.

WARRANT   An option to purchase a stated number of shares at a specified price within a specfic time frame. Warrants are typically offered as sweeteners to enhance the marketability of stock or debt issues.

WORKING CAPITAL   The difference between current assets and current liabilities.

YIELD   An investor's return on investment from its interest or dividend paying capability.

ZERO COUPON   A bond selling at a discount to maturity value and earning interest over the life of the bond but paying it upon maturity.

index

TWO GREAT
INVESTMENT OFFERS!!!

1. *Gaming & Investments Quarterly* covering the explosive gambling, hotel and entertainment industries with in-depth analysis of unique common stock investment opportunities.

Regularly $75.00 annual subscription.
Specially priced at $25.00 annual subscription.

2. *Utility & Energy Portfolio.* Each issue packed with attractive common stock investment opportunities, discussions of where to find higher yields and safety plus coverage of major industry trends and key players.

Regularly $95.00 annual subscription includes annual investment roundup of every major U.S. utility.
Specially priced at $35.00 annual subscription.

BONUS . . . Either subscription entitles you to a free copy of *Wall Street Words: The Basics and Beyond* by Richard J. Maturi, a $14.95 value.

Please send check or money order to: OR use your Discover® Card:

R. Maturi, Incorporated   Account No.:_____
1320 Curt Gowdy Drive
Cheyenne, WY 82009   Expiration Date:_____

                                 Signature: _____

_____ *Gaming and Investments Quarterly* @ $25.00. **SAVE $50.00!**

_____ *Utility and Energy Portfolio* @ $35.00. **SAVE $60.00!**

Name_____

Street _____

City _____ State _____ Zip_____

Phone ( )_____